Praise for
What Made Me Who I Am

"When a legend of an industry writes a book, you take notice. Bernie Swain, founder of the nation's top lecture agency, recounts the watershed moments of a number of well-known clients. *What Made Me Who I Am* is an insightful guide to what has empowered a generation of leaders. It's also full of fresh, moving stories that will help you navigate your life and challenges—no matter where or who you are."

—AMY CUDDY, Harvard Business School professor
and *New York Times* bestselling author of *Presence*

"Imagine having a backstage pass to the most interesting stages of the past three decades. Bernie Swain didn't just have that seat; he built the stage. In this inspiring book, he convinced many of the great leaders of our time to share the key turning points in their lives. It's like 34 autobiographies in one volume—full of delightful stories, surprising insights, and practical wisdom."

—ADAM GRANT, Wharton professor
and *New York Times* bestselling author of *Originals* and *Give and Take*

"Bernie Swain's *What Made Me Who I Am* is a treasure. By revealing the core motivations of some of our most powerful leaders, the book challenges all of us to push back our own frontiers and become better versions of ourselves. Prepare to be surprised, inspired, and—most of all—changed."

—DANIEL H. PINK, *New York Times* bestselling author
of *Drive, A Whole New Mind*, and *To Sell Is Human*

"Rarely do we get intimate profiles of so many outstanding leaders as we do in *What Made Me Who I Am*. Author Bernie Swain, a legend in the speaking world, reveals his clients' most personal leadership struggles alongside his own. Leaders at every level will see themselves in his frank, true-to-life tales about risk, tough times, and resilience. You'll also get some powerful inspiration and practical advice that could make a real difference for the rest of your life."

—STEPHEN M. R. COVEY, *New York Times* bestselling author
of *The Speed of Trust* and *Smart Trust*

"The stories in *What Made Me Who I Am* are both heartfelt and inspiring. The trust and confidence these famous names have in Bernie Swain is obvious on every page because they reveal to him intimate details of their lives that give real insight into how they became who they are today. Plus it is a fast and fun read."

—MAUREEN ORTH, Award-winning journalist
and special correspondent for *Vanity Fair*

"History is composed of the stories we tell; their turning points often have the power to inspire. From the personal trials of some of today's most iconic leaders, Bernie Swain has created an inspiring gem."

—KEN BURNS, Renowned filmmaker, including *The Civil War* and *Baseball*

"Everyone starts somewhere, and some of the most successful people of our times started in circumstances that were light years away from the lofty peaks they reached. Bernie Swain's book shares the stories of some of the successful individuals with whom he's worked—and the pivotal moments that proved life changing. You'll look at the events in your *own* life differently after reading about the lives of these leaders."

—DEBORAH NORVILLE, Anchor of *Inside Edition*
and *New York Times* bestselling author of *Thank You Power*

"We all have moments when we decide our fate—when we face down a problem, for example, or take a big risk. *What Made Me Who I Am* focuses on those inflection points for 34 notable people. You learn what has made all the difference in each of their lives and how these influences continue to drive them forward. This is an important book with great meaning for the rising generation."

—EUGENE ROBINSON, Pulitzer Prize–winning columnist
for *The Washington Post* and MSNBC analyst

"I love *What Made Me Who I Am* simply because Bernie Swain understands what moves people. You'll see yourself in every story, and you'll be inspired to take charge of your problems and opportunities in fresh, new ways."

—KATIE COURIC, Award-winning journalist
and *New York Times* bestselling author

"I've always believed that the most effective leaders are as generous as they are ambitious. They are at their best when they bring about the best in everyone they encounter. This book confirms that belief. In a true act of generosity, Bernie Swain has persuaded many of the remarkable thinkers, statesmen, and executives with whom he has worked to share the secrets of their success. The stories are larger than life, but their lessons may change *your* life. *What Made Me Who I Am* will help make you what you hope to become."

—WILLIAM C. TAYLOR, *Fast Company* cofounder
and *New York Times* bestselling author including *Simply Brilliant*

"Every human life is unique and unrepeatable. What we do and what we become in our lives has everything to do with whether we discover our personal talents and passions and have the determination to pursue them. What does that take and what happens when we do? In this compelling collection of powerful stories, Bernie Swain explores these fundamental questions through the lives of 34 extraordinary people in many different fields. No matter who you are, or what stage of life you've reached, you'll find *What Made Me Who I Am is* a treasure trove of insights and experiences on leadership, life, and achievement."

—SIR KEN ROBINSON, *New York Times* bestselling author
of *The Element: How Finding Your Passion Changes Everything*

"Bernie Swain—who has worked with US presidents, executives, and public figures for 35 years—gives us a rare look at the private moments that have helped determine the achievements of some of today's most compelling leaders. *What Made Me Who I Am* will remind you of the tremendous power of human potential, and that we are all in the people business."

—JOHN WREN, President and CEO, Omnicom Group

"Here's the truth in *What Made Me Who I Am*: Your future is in your hands—regardless of your circumstances. Get a copy. You'll be newly motivated to have more of a positive influence, get ahead, and expand your role in the world."

—DAN SCHAWBEL, Partner at Future Workplace
and author including the *New York Times* bestseller *Promote Yourself*

"Great people are sometimes born and sometimes made. But either way, great people are those who take charge of their potential. Bernie Swain's insightful book delivers first-hand accounts of how 34 of this generation's stars did just that—facing down problems, taking on risk, and persevering through tough challenges. *What Made Me Who I Am* is a terrific read for anyone who wants to make the most of what they have, and become all they can be."

—JACK AND SUZY WELCH, Business leaders
and *New York Times* bestselling authors including *The Real-Life MBA*

"Behind every president, CEO, Hollywood actor, or successful entrepreneur you'll find a person who's rarely talked about. Don't be surprised if that person's name is Bernie Swain. In his remarkable book *What Made Me Who I Am*, Swain shares a fascinating insight into some of the world's most admired individuals and how they in turn shaped equally remarkable individuals. *What Made Me Who I Am* is a must-read for anyone who aspires to reach for the stars—and have fun at the same time."

—MARTIN LINDSTROM, *New York Times* bestselling author
of *Buyology* and *Small Data*

"Bernie Swain has a compelling personal story and an incredibly unique vantage point on life. This book gathers it all together in powerful short profiles; read them and be inspired, entertained, and delighted."

—RORY VADEN, *New York Times* bestselling author
of *Take the Stairs* and *Procrastinate on Purpose*

"Bernie Swain has written a deeply insightful book, capturing the moments that turned ordinary people into today's heroes. *What Made Me Who I Am* is to be treasured."

—MARSHALL GOLDSMITH, *New York Times* bestselling author
including *Triggers*

"Everyone carries with them a lasting lesson that defines them. Bernie Swain has done a masterful job capturing the moments that have become lasting lessons for so many of today's greatest leaders."

—Luke Russert, Correspondent, NBC News

"Bernie Swain has created the perfect book for every bedside. When he called his friends of many years and asked them to tell their personal stories, they responded with warm, revealing tales—stories that are charming, often humorous, and inspiring. No wonder Bernie's clients are favorites of audiences all over the world."

—David Gergen, Political analyst, advisor to four US presidents, and Harvard Kennedy School professor

"The most unexpected moment can change your life, but only if you're paying attention. Bernie's terrific new book captures the real-life turning points of productive heroes—each one his friend. Who grabbed the opportunity, got competitive, and leaped forward? Learn from the best in *What Made Me Who I Am*."

—Barbara Corcoran, Shark investor on ABC's *Shark Tank*, and *New York Times* bestselling author

Contents

INTRODUCTION

A PREPOSTEROUS IDEA

In the lives of truly successful and accomplished people, you will often find a turning point. It may be a person in their life, a moment in time, or an unexpected event. It may be more intangible, such as the expectations set by others, or something that totally surprises you. But success and accomplishment don't happen in a vacuum; they rise from experiences that have a profound and lasting influence.

When you ask these successful and accomplished individuals about their turning points and listen carefully, you will often hear truly enlightening and inspirational stories—stories that can serve as a shining beacon of light to us all.

I learned this over a period of twenty-five years while founding and building our business, the Washington Speakers Bureau. We represented some of the biggest names in world leadership—among them, three of the past four presidents of the United States, the last four prime ministers of Great Britain, five secretaries of state, countless government and military leaders, journalists, authors, and sports legends. Throughout the course of my career, we shared much time and many experiences together. In our conversations, those we represented spoke often of the powerful influences and defining moments in their lives. These were the turning points they experienced that they rarely talked about in their speeches and appearances, stories that caused me to reconsider my own life and reflect on what I was hearing.

I credit Alex Haley, the author of *Roots* and one of the most compelling people that we've had the privilege to represent, for helping me to see that all these stories should be a book—this book. One day in the late eighties, Alex showed up at our office unannounced. He was like that—even though he was at the height of his fame and one of the best-known writers in the country, he would just walk into our offices and sit with us for an hour or more, talking and sharing stories.

On this occasion, Alex repeated one of his favorite sayings: "When an old person dies, it's like a library burning." That pithy phrase stuck with me, and as the days and months passed, I began to understand what he was telling me. Each life—the ones recounted here, the millions that go uncelebrated—is defined by experiences that have volumes to teach us. Each life is a storehouse of wisdom and knowledge, its own library, stuffed to the rafters.

I wrote this book for two reasons: To share with you a collection of stories that have inspired me for many years and taught me something about life, the stories of a compelling and eclectic group of my friends who were guided by their powerful influences and defining moments. And, by my recounting these stories, to give you a better picture and understanding of your own life, and the importance of your turning points in the process.

Many names will be familiar. You've read about them, seen them at press conferences, on news broadcasts, on playing fields. You probably know what they've accomplished and why they're famous. CNN and Wikipedia can tell you. The stories they shared with me and I recall in this book reveal something more personal and relevant—what makes us who we are.

My front row seat to the worldwide lecture circuit has provided me with a lifetime of insight and inspiration. It began and unfolded like the stories in this book. I was in my early thirties and just months away from becoming the athletic director at George Washington University when a friend's half serious note spurred my wife, Paula, and me to abandon our careers and risk our family's future on a preposterous idea. Our friend Harry Rhoads had sent us an article from *Fortune* magazine, entitled "Speech is Golden on the Lecture Circuit," about the Harry Walker Agency in New York, then the world's largest lecture agency. In the article, Henry Kissinger was quoted as asking Walker why he should sign with his company instead of with one of his competitors. Walker's response: "We don't have any competitors."

Harry taped a note to the page. It read: "No competitors?" Paula took the note as an invitation and a challenge. I thought she was kidding. Weeks later, Paula's simple but passionate argument—that every life, even ours, needs a great if totally unpredictable and crazy adventure—prevailed and I gave in. With no experience or real plan (but with a one-year-old baby), we quit our jobs, ended our careers, and started a lecture agency with Harry.

Our first office was, quite literally, a closet. It held the office supplies for Chuck Hagel—who would become US secretary of defense—and his business partner (and our friend) Bill Collins. The three of us shared two small desks and two telephones. When Chuck and Bill's staff needed stationery supplies, they walked into our closet/office. When we needed to leave our office, even to use the restroom, we sometimes had to wait until one of Chuck's meetings was over.

For months, we sat in our closet hoping that someone would call us. But no one ever did. As it turned out, Harry Walker's claim of "no competitors" was a strategic boast, a way of separating himself from other agencies. There were dozens of lecture agencies up and down the East Coast representing all kinds of famous people. We were clueless. There was, after all, no Internet in 1980 to save us from our decisions.

Sitting in our closet late at night, I would often close my eyes, shake my head, and ask myself, "What have we done?"

A year later, little had changed. Harry Walker and the other big agencies still controlled the industry. Most of the famous speakers remained under written contracts with those agencies. Our office was still a closet, and we didn't represent anyone. Only one thing had changed. We had spent all our savings on supplies, rent, mailing lists, brochures, and direct mailings that had little or no effect, and we were out of money.

Then, just as we were about to close our closet door, we got our first exclusive speaker—Steve Bell, anchorman for ABC's *Good Morning America*. I had helped Steve get access to the GWU swimming pool for a news story years before, and he had just left his old agency. When he called us, we were so excited and anxious that we simply sealed the deal with a quick handshake and no paperwork. "If someone is unhappy with us," I justified after the handshake, "what good will it be holding him to a signed piece of paper?"

This questionable decision turned out to be a "defining moment" strategy for our new little company. Word spread in the small, news-driven town of Washington. Knowing they could walk out on us at any time, a surprising number of speakers, mostly Washington journalists (including Hugh Sidey, Carl Rowan, Robert Novak, and Mark Shields) gave us a chance. Knowing we could lose them at any time, we worked hard to keep our clients happy.

For the next seven years, we did what many start-ups must do to succeed. We arrived to work every day at dawn, we didn't leave the office until late at night, we obsessed about every small detail, and we learned from our mistakes. There were no vacations; we often worked seven days a week. We were driven, always thinking, planning, and rethinking, but most importantly, we were networking intensely and building relationships.

Thankfully, it started to pay off. We added another impressive list of speakers, which is what most distinguishes one agency from another, among them Peter Jennings, Art Buchwald, Charles Kuralt, David Brinkley, George Will, Lou Holtz, Jim Valvano, and Terry

Bradshaw. We eventually moved to new offices, got health insurance (just in time for the birth of our three-month-premature, two-pound baby girl), and hired what was the start of a very talented staff and team of agents that would fully develop in the decade to follow. For the first time, we could favorably compare our success recruiting talent (speakers) and booking events against much of our competition. I'm not sure Harry Walker took much notice of us, but in just seven productive and foundation-making years, our reputation in the industry and roster of speakers was strong.

The big turning point came in 1988, when we received an invitation to the White House. Ronald Reagan would be leaving office in a few months, and he was looking for an agency to book and manage his speaking engagements. We got invited to interview.

There were dozens of agencies in the running, including large East Coast companies that specialized in politicians and Hollywood agencies that Reagan knew from his acting career. The president's staff conducted the initial interviews, and although we knew the field of potential agencies was being narrowed, we remained totally in the dark. Unlike almost every other thing going on in Washington, there were no rumors to shed light on their thinking. All we knew was that the top two choices of the staff would be presented to the president and First Lady, and they would make the final decision.

I don't think anyone in Washington, or elsewhere for that matter, thought we would be the agency selected to represent Ronald Reagan, and yet we were optimistic. There's a confidence you get over time when you build something of your own and, after years of surviving the early days and then thriving on later challenges, we were confident. But that optimism was challenged when we heard nothing for two months, not a word. Then out of the blue, my secretary buzzed me in the office: "Fred Ryan is on the phone for you." Fred was Reagan's chief of staff and now publisher of the *Washington Post*. I held my breath and took the call, braced for bad news. Fred got right to the point: "Bernie, President and Mrs. Reagan have selected you to represent them." It was that simple, and yet breathtaking. Trying not to sound too excited or unprofessional, I thanked him, assured him that we would do a good job, and hung up the phone.

Superstitious and worried that the decision was somehow a mistake, we refused to ask how it all happened. But then one day in our office, I blurted out the question to Fred Ryan. "You actually came in second; Harry Walker was first," he said. Time stood still and I barely heard the next few sentences. "But, it was the president himself who chose you. He liked that you, Paula, and Harry were starting up a new business, and he wanted to give you a chance."

I sat in my office that day thinking how totally amazing it was that a president would trust his legacy to a fledgling agency and a small, inexperienced group of people. But, as the years passed, I came to understand why it made perfect sense. Reagan was, at heart, a small-town boy who believed in entrepreneurship and the little guy. Like the people whose stories are in this book, he was guided by and true to the powerful influences and defining moments that formed and shaped his life.

With the president's decision, our lives were to change like we'd never imagined. Twenty-one months later, Margaret Thatcher, at the recommendation of President Reagan, asked us to represent her without meeting us. Then, General Norman Schwarzkopf called us from his bunker near the end of the Gulf War. Over time, we were representing George H. W. Bush, Colin Powell, Madeleine Albright, Tony Blair, Condoleezza Rice, Rudy Giuliani, Bob Gates, and so many others. The roster of clients we would eventually represent, it was said, became the greatest in history since the very first agency, the Redpath Bureau, represented Mark Twain, Ralph Waldo Emerson, Susan B. Anthony, Frederick Douglass, and other notables of the post–Civil War era.

If you'd told me in my twenties that I would play a part, even this small part, in the lives of presidents, prime ministers, and great achievers of all kinds, I might have questioned your sanity. But it was real, and not only did we represent these famous individuals as clients, we soon got to know them and, over time, earned their trust and friendship (the key to our success). In this book, I'll share with you what my conversations with my friends taught me: the powerful influences and defining moments, the turning points in our lives, don't just change us, but they can make us stronger and wiser, and contribute greatly to our character and accomplishment.

The storytellers whose journeys I will recount and narrate in this book stand as an assembly of individuals who defined their generation. Here, they share the moments that defined them. Bob Woodward finds his passion for investigative journalism while working as a janitor. Condoleezza Rice's life path is set by her grandfather's controversial decision over a hundred years ago. Tony Blair's journey to becoming prime minister is almost derailed by Mick Jagger. Robert Reich's childhood friend's death sends him on a life mission to change the world.

These stories, about extraordinary people who often started from humble and modest beginnings, will surprise you. Some may even move you. My genuine hope is that you will see yourself in many of these stories and they will inspire you to recognize and learn from the turning points in your life. They did that for me.

MADELEINE ALBRIGHT

Before Madeleine Albright was confirmed as the first female US secretary of state, there were many people who thought a woman wouldn't be able to negotiate with Arab countries. But she told me once that she actually had more trouble with American men. She had been around Washington for a while, and many of the men in her circle knew her either as a friend of their wives or someone they'd sat next to at a dinner party. Some of them had a hard time, she recalled, making the leap from carpool mom to secretary of state.

It wasn't what I expected, but the defining moments and influences that Madeleine shared with me over the years centered on the theme of parent/child relationships and how they shape us. As she talked about her life, it reconfirmed what has crossed my mind many times—that we grow up, become our own person, and still, for many of us, the powerful urge to make our parents happy remains.

I was born in Prague in 1937, when the Czechoslovak nation was less than two decades old. At the time of my birth, my father, Josef, was a young press attaché stationed in Belgrade, Yugoslavia. He came from a family of businessmen, but he wanted to be a diplomat; he had an instinct for civility and cooperation. He had studied at Charles University in Prague, which was founded in 1348, and then at the Sorbonne in Paris. A passionate Czechoslovak patriot, my father was a remarkable man and the most important influence on my life. It was his clearheaded and fair-minded character that saw me through an unsettled, even tumultuous childhood, and that set a standard I have endeavored to live up to ever since.

In September 1938, when I was still a toddler, the Munich Agreement was signed by Germany, France, England, and Italy. It allowed Germany to annex the largely German-speaking northern part of Czechoslovakia and was widely regarded as an act of appeasement toward Adolf Hitler. Soon thereafter my father was recalled from his position in Yugoslavia. I didn't find out why until years later, but it turns out my mother, Anna, was indirectly responsible. She was a smart, vivacious woman, charming and fun, but very outspoken. She was furious that Czechoslovakia wasn't a participant in the conference that negotiated the agreement and that it accepted the annexation without a fight. At a dinner party, she announced that she would "rather marry a street sweeper than a soldier who didn't fight." Her indiscretion was reported to the Czechoslovak government, which was under the influence of the Germans. Soon thereafter, my father was recalled from his post.

We were living in Prague in March of 1939 when the Nazis marched into the city. A Czechoslovak government in exile was established in London, and we moved to England so that my father could be part of it. He took a prominent role in countering German propaganda, including participating in BBC radio broadcasts to Czechoslovakia. I remember listening to his voice on the radio and being awed by his intelligence and passion. It's safe to say that he became my hero.

My early years were deeply influenced by the tense atmosphere in Europe and then by the war itself. Before we moved to the English countryside, we were in the middle of the Blitz, with bombs dropping all around us, and I spent many hours in underground air-raid shelters. These were serious times, and my parents cared deeply about democracy, morality, and human rights. After we had moved to the country, my father walked me to school every day before catching the train to London. As we walked, he would encourage me to do my best in school, and in life, and to always treat people with respect.

After the war ended, we moved back to Prague, and my father was named ambassador to Yugoslavia. These years were the first stable ones of my childhood, and life in the embassy was comfortable, with a cook, maids, and a chauffeur. We were in Belgrade for three years when my father was named the Czechoslovak representative to the United Nations to deal with the issue of India and Pakistan over Kashmir.

Then the communists took over in Czechoslovakia. My father had no interest in being part of that government, so he defected to the United States, where he asked for, and was granted, political asylum for himself and his family. At that time, the Rockefeller Foundation was helping political exiles find jobs that suited their talents. While diplomacy was his first love, that wasn't an option. With the foundation's help, he found a job teaching international relations at the University of Denver.

My father was a serious man, with a far-ranging intellect, but there were other sides of his nature. He loved to sing and play the piano and to spend time playing with me and my younger sister and brother. Every night, all of us sat down to dinner together, and the topic of conversation inevitably turned to foreign affairs. Although our lives had been nomadic, my parents maintained a consistency that made it all seem normal.

We were living in faculty housing at the university, which was quite a step down from an ambassador's residence. The house was small and cramped, and we children had the first-floor bedrooms. My parents slept in the basement, where my father set up a makeshift study. There was one problem: the basement flooded constantly. My father would sit at his desk, working away with his feet up on bricks. We all laughed about it, but it wasn't exactly the way you would visualize a former ambassador living. Again, my parents handled it with equanimity and grace; they simply carried on. It was a powerful lesson.

Of course, there were times when I was a bit embarrassed by my father. Although we lived in America, he remained an Old World European in many ways. But he also wanted to fit in. So, since he was in Colorado, he took up fishing—wearing a coat and tie. There he was, looking like the very model of a European diplomat—tailored suit, combed-back hair, wire-rim glasses, and a pipe—casting his rod. As for me, I just wanted to be an ordinary American teenager.

My English elementary school awarded honor points—for grades, sports, behavior, and community service. Whenever I got a point, I would come home and tell my parents and they were thrilled. So I started telling them I'd won points when I hadn't. Of course, each point had to have a story behind it. One day, I came home and claimed that I'd pulled a teacher out of a rosebush and been awarded multiple points for my bravery and dexterity. Then I upped the ante by claiming that I'd won so many points that the school was going to award me its ultimate accolade, the Egyptian Cup.

The cup, of course, was another figment of my parent-pleasing imagination. My father, who I suspect was on to me by this time, kept asking me when I would be bringing home the vaunted Egyptian Cup. Cornered, I switched directions. I was soon losing points, unfairly of course, for minor infractions. I was being singled out, bullied. Why, one teacher had even made me sit on needles. That was the last straw for my mother, who announced she was going to march down to the school in the morning and demand that this mistreatment cease immediately. At that point, I had no choice but to come clean. From then on, whenever I said something fishy, my father would ask, "So, where's the Egyptian Cup?"

I continued in Denver public schools for seventh and eighth grades. Then I got a scholarship to a private girls' school. I didn't want to accept it, but my father insisted. There were sixteen girls in my class, and they were all from wealthy families. We didn't belong to the country club. I was intimidated at first, but my parents had given me the great gift of confidence. While I couldn't compete with my classmates for best dressed, I knew that my parents were smart and read a great deal, that my father had authored books and had served his country.

When I was a sophomore in high school, I won a United Nations essay contest and I also formed an international relations club. I was trying to be the perfect daughter. I'm still trying. I was going through my papers recently, and I found an essay I'd written in high school about Mohandas Gandhi. I'm sure I picked the topic because my father had served in India as a diplomat, and I wanted to please him. Later, my father wrote extensively about the communist takeover in Czechoslovakia. Need I say what the topic of my honor thesis at Wellesley was?

When it came to dating, my father was very strict. When a boy came to pick me up, he and my mother would make comments in Czech, sizing him up. The poor boy, of course, had no idea what they were saying. Then my father would get in the family car and follow us to the dance or party or movie. When he saw we had safely arrived, he would drive home. Hours later, when the boy and I left wherever we were, we'd find my father sitting patiently in the car at the curb, waiting to escort us home. He would then invite my date to come in for milk and cookies. I didn't have a lot of second dates until I got to college.

My parents came to love America deeply; they were very grateful to be here. My father's favorite statement was, "Nothing makes me happier than to be a professor in a free country." He loved teaching, loved his students, and loved to make foreign affairs come alive in the classroom. Condoleezza Rice studied with him, and she credits him as having a strong influence on her thinking and maturation.

After college, I married, worked as a journalist, had three daughters, and earned advanced degrees in foreign relations, before being nominated and confirmed 99–0 by the United States Senate as secretary of state.

Today, I'm busier than ever, teaching, writing, and being a grandmother. Through it all, I've felt that my father was with me, perched on my shoulder, still following me around, inspiring me. The volatile politics of Eastern Europe short-circuited his diplomatic career. That has always been on my mind and I hope in some small way, I've made him proud. Being secretary of state is a challenging experience. But I never had any trouble staying focused. I just had to picture my father in his flooded basement study, working away with his feet up on bricks.

DAVE BARRY

Sometimes, the joke is on the jokester. In 1988, the Miami Herald *played a prank on humorist Dave Barry, the author and nationally syndicated columnist. On his way to Key West with his eight-year-old son Rob, Barry got a call from his editor asking him to drop by the office to discuss a story. When he arrived, he found everyone gathered in the newsroom for the announcement that he had won the Pulitzer Prize. Noticing the disappointment on his son's face because their trip together would be cancelled, Dave whispered in Rob's ear, "I'll buy you a Nintendo game." Rob immediately jumped into the arms of his father as someone took a picture. The next day it ran on the front page of the* Herald *with everyone commenting on how excited the boy had been for his father. The joke was, Barry would recall, that young Rob was just in the throes of Nintendo fever.*

I've always wondered how people with distinctive personalities, in Dave's case those who make us laugh, got to be that way. In recalling the powerful influences in his life, Dave tells his secret: humor, like our individual differences in the way we think, feel, and behave, comes in great part from the strong and sometimes profound impressions made on us when we are very young.

My mother, Marion, was the funniest person I've ever known. She passed away in 1987, and, in the years since, I've come to realize just how hilarious and edgy she was. Growing up with her, I

7

took her skewered point of view for granted, and when I went out into the world, I was surprised to learn that most people didn't see things the way Mom did. She picked up on the odd side of, well, just about everything.

I had two brothers and a sister, and in the Barry household, we didn't compete on the basis of academic or athletic achievement—it was all about who could make everyone laugh. We didn't take anything or anyone too seriously, including ourselves.

I grew up in the New York suburb of Armonk in the 1950s. Dad took the train to work; Mom was a housewife. She cooked our meals, did the laundry, and drove us everywhere. She had an incredibly dry, sometimes dark, sense of humor. For example, one summer day, my sister Kate and I set off to go swimming in a pond near our house. Mom opened the kitchen window and called out, in her best June Cleaver voice, "Don't drown, kids." And we answered, "We won't, Mom." Some people would have found that exchange alarming; we found it hilarious.

Mom did all her errands in Armonk Village, which was full of mom-and-pop stores. One day I was with her at Bricetti's Market, surrounded by other 1950s mothers. Ray Bricetti asked from behind the counter, "How are you doing today, Marion?" Mom answered, "Just shitty, Ray." The other customers gasped. I thought it was hilarious, as did Ray. Housewives weren't supposed to talk like that back then.

My father, David, also had a terrific sense of humor and intro-duced me to my favorite humorists. I probably ended up being a writer because I was exposed to Robert Benchley, P. G. Wodehouse, Art Buchwald, and Max Shulman. Dad had a dry, subtle wit, and a wonderful sense of the absurd. The combination of Mom's edgy, fear-less humor and Dad's more low-key wit shaped and defined me.

At school, I used humor to make myself popular. It didn't always work, especially with the teachers. I was a wiseass and, if there was a particularly uptight teacher, I was likely to mouth off. I spent my share of time in detention. What can I say? I was this dweeby little guy and being funny helped me win acceptance. In fact, I was elected class clown of Pleasantville High School's class of 1965. That's my earliest major achievement in the field of humor.

Mom's humor masked some pain. She was a troubled person, unhappy in many ways, and she saw a psychiatrist later in life. But she never lost her sense of humor. In 1984, my father died after a long struggle with heart disease. He was a much-loved Presbyterian minister and social worker in New York City. After the service, my brothers, sister, and I went to the cemetery with Mom, who was carrying Dad's ashes in a cardboard box. We placed them in the hole that had been dug and said a few words. We all cried. Then, as we were leaving, Mom read a nearby gravestone: "So that's why we don't see him around anymore." All of a sudden we were all laughing and crying at the same time.

Mom was straightforward and unpretentious. My Dad was from Kansas, so the two of them were very midwestern. Neither had any patience for hypocrisy or snobbery.

Dad ran an organization called the New York City Mission Society, which operated programs for inner-city kids, overwhelmingly black and Puerto Rican. They also ran a summer camp in upstate New York. My siblings and I all went to the camp, which we loved. Armonk was pretty much all white. Then in the summer we would go off to camp and find ourselves in the minority.

I always wanted to be a writer. I wrote for the high school newspaper and the college paper during my four years at Haverford. After graduating, I went to work as a reporter for a small-town Pennsylvania daily. I never thought I'd be able to make a living as a humorist. Then I moved to the Associated Press, and after that I left journalism and taught writing seminars at big companies. Basically, I would get a bunch of people in a room and try to get them to use fewer, less pretentious words. Usually I failed.

By then I was in my thirties. I was writing a weekly humor column that ran in the small paper where I had started my career. They paid me $23 per column. I wasn't wildly ambitious, I had my column, and I was feeding my family by teaching the ineffective writing courses.

Then I got the classic big break. When my son Rob was born, I wrote a comic essay on natural childbirth, which was all the rage among yuppie baby boomers. I mocked it because it turned out to be so different from what my wife and I had been taught in the natural childbirth classes we'd taken. The essay was picked up by the *Philadelphia Inquirer*'s Sunday magazine. I guess it struck a nerve because just about every paper in the country reprinted it. Suddenly I was in demand as a humor writer. The *Miami Herald* offered me a job, and I'm still there.

I've always viewed my job sort of like a magician or a stand-up comic. My talent is for entertaining people, not analyzing issues. I've never felt qualified to tell people what to think. I've sometimes felt guilty about that because Dad was involved in so many good works. He was a much better person than me.

One of the highlights of my life was playing in a band called the Rock Bottom Remainders, which raised over $2 million for literacy-related causes. My bandmates were fellow writers, including Stephen King, Scott Turow, Mitch Albom, Ridley Pearson, Roy Blount Jr., Greg Iles, and Amy Tan. We were joined at one time or another by Bruce Springsteen, Roger McGuinn, and Warren Zevon. Springsteen told us, "Your band's not too bad. It's not too good either. Don't let it get any better, otherwise you'll just be another lousy band." I used to say we played music as well as Metallica wrote books. Mom probably just would have said, "You suck."

TONY BLAIR

A story that Tony Blair loves to tell reveals just how polite the British can be—even when engaged in the hand-to-hand combat of politics. When Blair was running for his second term as prime minister of the United Kingdom, his two eldest sons, Euan and Nicky, helped out by canvassing London neighborhoods and encouraging residents to vote. At one neighborhood visit, the owner of the house, not recognizing Nicky, lambasted the prime minister, saying, "Tony Blair is the worst prime minister England has ever had." Upon leaving and spotting his brother Euan, Nicky said, "Euan, go to that house, that man really loves Dad." When Euan heard the same complaints from the same man, he could not help himself. "Stop it, that is my dad you are talking about." Without skipping a beat, the homeowner said, "Oh, oh he is not really that bad. Want to come in for a cup of tea?"

The turning points of his life that Tony shared reminded me, in part, of the famous John Donne poem "No Man Is an Island." As we go through life, charting our own individual path, our lives are not solo acts. Tony helped me see that, in life, some of us are destined to complete the unfulfilled dreams of others.

As a child, I was mischievous and even rebellious. I was always getting in trouble, staying out later than I was allowed, being cheeky in class, that sort of thing. I was a baby boomer, part of the sixties generation, and I can easily imagine I might have become a real rebel and gotten into real trouble. But when I was ten, the seminal event in my young life occurred and changed me forever.

First, a little background. I was born in Edinburgh. My dad, Leo, had been a foster child, and he grew up in a very poor and tough part of Glasgow. His father worked as a rigger on ships and as a clerk in an office, but was often unemployed and the family struggled. In addition, my dad was only five foot four inches tall, which led to considerable teasing. He had a lot of charm and discipline, though, and he was determined to get out of that neighborhood. He studied hard and got grades high enough to qualify for university. Then he was called to service in World War II. He went into the army as a private and came out a major.

After the war, Dad met and married my mother, Hazel. She was from a Northern Irish family that had moved to Glasgow. Her father was a butcher. She was a pretty redhead, just a lovely woman and a terrific mother. I found out later just how much steel she had in her spine.

There were great changes afoot in the world after the war. Young men had seen the unspeakable, and women had entered the work-force in unprecedented numbers. Winston Churchill had led England through the conflict, and yet he lost his bid for reelection in 1945. At first look, it seems ungrateful of the nation, but Churchill represented the old-fashioned way of doing things, and the people at the time wanted to forge the world in their own image. Many Brits, who were Conservatives at the start of the war, were Labour when it was over. People from all classes worked side by side on the home front and fought side by side in the trenches, and that experience changed minds and hearts.

My father, however, went into the war as a socialist and came out a Conservative. He was a striver. I think he identified with those above him and aspired to reach that level. He went on to university and became a barrister and a lecturer. He was a marvelous speaker, artic-ulate and stirring. Then he got interested in politics. By the time I was ten years old, he had accomplished many of his goals and was about to stand for Parliament from a Conservative constituency. Everyone thought he had a great political career ahead of him.

One day I came home from school to find out that he had suffered a stroke and was in the hospital. He almost died, was paralyzed on one side, and couldn't speak. He was only forty years old. I was devastated, but my mother's example guided me.

My father was in the hospital for months. When he came home, all he could do was ask for a cup of tea, which is very British, and say, "Good." My mother sat by his bedside, day in and day out. She basically taught Dad how to speak again—slowly, painstakingly, word by word. Mom was amazing, and she inspired me. I learned that one must never, ever give up. It took three years, but her devotion and determination paid off. Dad was able to go back to work and complete his career as a judge. But his political career was over before it started.

Ironically, in some way, Dad's stroke was a blessing for me. It forced me to grow up. I had been a rebellious child—difficult, a troublemaker at school. I think if my father had gone on to become really successful I might well have taken a different path in life. In the sixties, there was a lot of drug use and mindless rebellion. I could easily have become a casualty of those forces.

Dad's stroke taught me that life is tougher than I'd thought. I was in private school in Edinburgh, and, given our situation, I had to apply for a scholarship. It was humiliating, and I felt vulnerable. I understood, on a visceral level, what it means to struggle. From that time on, I gained a sense of urgency and determination. I admired my father enormously. He'd pulled himself up from difficult circumstances. I wanted to make him proud, to emulate his example. Suddenly, indulging my whims and having a good time seemed far less important. I felt a deep obligation to fulfill my potential.

In the years before his stroke, music was one of Dad's great passions. When we had guests, he would invariably end up at the piano, which he had taught himself to play. This made a deep impression on me—the pleasure that music brought him and his listeners filled the house and lifted everyone's spirits.

After I finished high school, I impulsively decided to spend a year in London pursuing a music career. It was the height of the swinging sixties. I'd only been to London once, on a very brief visit. I hitchhiked down from Edinburgh with five pounds in my pocket. I had one contact, a friend of a friend, and I went and knocked on his door. No answer. I ended up spending that first night on a park bench; fortunately it was summer. Then I got a job in a music store and made enough to rent a room.

Pretty soon I met some fellows who were interested in starting a band, and for a year I worked with them. You could call me their manager, but that sounds more professional than it was. We were a ragtag bunch, but I did get them some gigs. Then I started to sing and play a bit myself. But I'd promised my dad I would go to university, and after a year I did just that, enrolling at St John's, Oxford.

Even with a heavy study load, I kept up with the music at St John's—some classmates and I put together a band. It was standard rock and roll, and I loved it. Performing is a great lesson and discipline. You have to get up in front of a crowd and engage and entertain them. Just watching Mick Jagger, who made an indelible impression on me, is a lesson in the power of performance. I went to a lot of concerts. I saw the Rolling Stones, David Bowie, the Doobie Brothers, Lou Reed, and many more. The unity among rock fans transcended the songs. The music brought people together, which, I later realized, is what all good politicians strive to do.

I was the lead singer in our group, and I played a little guitar. A friend of mine who has been successful in the music business was recently asked what first attracted him to the industry; he answered: "Back in the sixties, a girl boasted to me that she'd been out with Paul McCartney's chauffeur's brother. I knew then and there it was the business for me."

I was actually somewhat serious about the music business. I had little interest in politics. Then I began to study law, and I became fascinated by the way the judicial system, and by extension government, works. This led me to public service. I suppose I wanted a steadier profession than music, and of course, I was motivated by the life of my father. So I cut my hair and put my energies into my studies. But the sense of performing, which is important in politics, stayed with me.

TERRY BRADSHAW

Terry Bradshaw once explained to me that quarterbacks can be endlessly competitive, even when off the field. Phil Robertson, future Duck Dynasty star, was the quarterback that Terry Bradshaw replaced at Louisiana Tech. Phil quit football because he loved fishing and duck hunting more than football. When Phil took Terry out on his boat fishing, he would put a cloth sack over Terry's head and make him lay facedown until they reached Phil's favorite fishing spot. Phil thought that if Terry saw the route, he would be there the next day, stealing all of his fish.

The moments in Terry's life that I recount here are a message about the lives we live. Sometimes we find ourselves living the life other people expect of us, but as Terry shows, we are happiest when we ignore the pressures and false expectations of others.

Draft day, 1970. I was walking out my front door, fishing pole in hand, when my dad stopped me and told me to get my sport coat. "The TV trucks are coming," he said. I stood there, not really sure what he was talking about. Back then, draft day wasn't the heavily scrutinized media event that it is today. At best, I thought I would go quietly in the third round to the New Orleans Saints and maybe get a small article in the local paper. But then I got a phone call telling me that the Pittsburgh Steelers had chosen me as the first pick of the draft. My first thought was, "Okay, great . . . where's Pittsburgh?" My second thought: "Didn't they have a terrible 1–13 record last year?"

I arrived in Pittsburgh and hit the ground stumbling. I was an immature kid of average intellect with simple ideas, terrible study habits, and limited social skills. I had no idea how serious professional football really was. I had spent the previous four years at Louisiana Tech University, and I loved it there. In fact, I never had more fun in my career than I did playing at Tech. All of the coaches and alumni treated me like family, and we played football with a pure love for the game. Plus, I loved the school's off-the-beaten-path country charm. I had grown up spending summers on my uncle's farm, roping and riding horses, going barefoot for days, so I loved the down-home country vibe of Tech. On off days, we'd go fishing or ride horses.

Needless to say, Pittsburgh was a world away from my life on the farm and at Tech. To make things worse, the Steelers coach, Chuck Noll, didn't even want to draft me—the owners made him do it. I just wasn't his kind of quarterback. He had a fairly simple offensive strategy, and I liked to mix things up. I also didn't study the way he wanted me to. At Louisiana Tech, I didn't have a quarterback coach, and there was no offensive coordinator. Playing within Pittsburgh's new framework felt like I was being reined in. It was an adjustment, a baptism by fire, and it rattled me. I threw and played erratically.

In my first game, we went up against the Houston Oilers. I was benched in the second half. In fact, that's how my first season progressed: I'd start a game, then get benched, then start again, then get benched. I'd sit there on the sidelines, miserable and misunderstood, wondering how the hell I ended up in this place.

Of course, it was largely my fault. Instead of trying to adjust, I rebelled. Being the number-one pick had swelled my head so big it forced the common sense out. If the coaches wanted me to go right, I ducked left. I pouted and felt sorry for myself and didn't do my homework. I dicked around in practice. I thought I could win games by myself.

The culture shock also hit me hard. I was a southern boy and hadn't done a lot of traveling. Even though I'd lived in a segregated society my entire life, I had grown up in a family that had no prejudices toward African Americans, and I saw black and white people coexisting all the time. But I had still never played alongside African American athletes. At Steelers team meals, black players ate on one side of the table and white players on the other. One afternoon, running back Frenchy Fuqua sat down on the white side and another black player said, "What are you doing, man? Get your ass up." Frenchy answered, "I'm sitting down to eat my lunch." Playing in Pittsburgh woke me up to how my innocent country attitude sometimes meant I was burying my head in the sand.

If I was going to survive, I had to grow up. I was a flat-out star at Louisiana Tech; in Pittsburgh, I was getting booed by fans. That pissed me off. And the media piled on, calling me a bumpkin with mush for brains. Suddenly the pressure, media spotlight, and expectations were turned up a thousand times, and it was more than I could handle. I became a recluse in my rental apartment. I was literally scared to go out, sure that fans would taunt me. They were expecting what I was expecting—that I was going to win football games. That wasn't happening, and I was retreating into a defensive crouch.

One night, I sat in front of my TV, crying my eyes out, filled with shame. I felt like I'd lost my way. I pleaded with God to help me—I wanted to hold my head up high on the field and off. I wanted to have some calmness and peace in my life. What came back to me was not a lightning bolt or *aha!* moment but a gentle voice telling me I needed to get real. Everybody faces trials in life, everyone is tested, and here I was, failing miserably and feeling sorry for myself. Did I want to be miserable and play poorly? Or did I want to start adjusting to the realities of being an NFL quarterback in a big northern city? Something in me told me that I had the key and title to my life, and shame on me if I allowed other people to steal that from me. I finished praying, I went to practice the next day, and I set out cultivating a new attitude.

Day by day, I learned to drop the attitude and to listen to my coach and my teammates. The media could be tough, but fighting them only intensified their attacks. So I learned to smile and defuse tension with humor. I would beat them to the punch by making fun of myself first. Most of all, I worked hard. By my second season, I was playing pretty well.

It wasn't all sugar and spice from there on out. Even after two Super Bowl wins, people treated me like some dumb quarterback. In Super Bowl XIII, we went up against the Dallas Cowboys, and Dallas linebacker Thomas "Hollywood" Henderson famously told reporters that I was "so dumb, [I] couldn't spell cat if you spotted [me] a C and an A." I'd just come off an amazing season, and here I was, answering the same old charge that I was some country idiot. Hollywood was trying to get in my head, and honestly, it was working.

Even as I made progress, nothing made me angrier more quickly than attacking my intellect. In high school, I had been offered a position at Louisiana State University, but the offer was contingent upon my passing the ACT test. I failed it—not once, but twice—and LSU told me I would have to go to a junior college before attending their school. No way, I thought. The experience turned out to be a blessing, as I went to and loved Louisiana Tech, but it still stuck with me. Whenever someone called me a "country bumpkin," that test score, and everything I felt it said about me, loomed large in my mind.

I didn't respond publicly to Hollywood Henderson's insult, but internally, I was seething. Furious. After years of playing professional football, I knew that the more emotionally involved and bothered I was, the worse I played. If I allowed myself to stay jacked up, I could cost my team the championship. I had spent so much of that season, and seasons before, learning how to find a peaceful place within myself, that place that was untouched by the criticism or reproach or fear. I would repeat the word "calm" to myself over and over. If I was going to win, I'd need to double-down my discipline to find that sacred relaxed space in my mind.

I'm proud to say that that game was one of the highlights of my career and life. I threw four touchdowns, passed for 318 yards (a career high for me), and helped our team win a very difficult 35–31 matchup. I consider that day a benchmark moment in my journey, and it wouldn't have been possible without my faith and my willingness to stand up to difficult trials instead of continuing to sulk.

Years later, I bumped into Hollywood Henderson at the Dallas airport. I had no idea what to expect, but he was very gracious and apologized for his comments and hugged me. That was a very moving moment for me. We go through life with these set ideas of who is with us or against us, but you just never know how life will surprise you.

I had a good run with the Steelers, and in 1983 it was time to move on, so I left the NFL. I don't like looking back too much, but if there is one fundamental lesson I learned in Pittsburgh, it was an echo of what the great philosopher Popeye once said: "I yam what I yam." When I showed up, I was filled with insecurity and hubris, desperate to prove myself as smart and talented yet too arrogant to put in the work. I wasn't one of these quarterbacks like Tom Brady or Peyton Manning who came in with the right attitude and confidence. That might have made my life easier, but it wasn't the journey I was on. I had to learn that it's okay to be yourself, to be real, because then you don't have to worry about convincing others that you're different.

Maybe I am just some innocent country boy who was never that bright. But I wouldn't trade my life for anything or anybody else's. A couple of months ago, I went to church out by my house in Hawaii. The church we go to is a couple hundred feet above the ocean, with palm trees swaying and a gentle breeze coming in an open door. Just like at home, you can walk in barefoot. I'd come thousands of miles, played in hundreds of games, failed, succeeded, and done it all over again. And I fought and stumbled my way to this little slice of heaven that reminded me in some ways of my uncle's farm. How lucky and blessed I am to live this life I can finally call my own.

TOM BROKAW

Tom Brokaw tends to be humble regarding his intelligence, often tell-ing this story about his alma mater. After Brokaw became the NBC Nightly News *anchor, Washington University in St. Louis called his college advisor at the University of South Dakota. "We'd like to know more about Tom's scholarship during his undergraduate days because we're giving him an honorary degree," they said. In an instant, the college advisor responded, "Well, we always thought the degree we gave him was an honorary degree."*

The part of his life Tom shared with me is a powerful public service announcement for mentors, and how they change lives. Certainly, this was Tom's experience and he shares the influences and defining moments that many of us, if we take notice, may find in our own lives.

I was born in 1940, a product of South Dakota, where my family's roots run deep. Both my parents came from rural, working-class backgrounds and grew up during the Depression. My mother, Jean Conley, lived on a farm where they mined gravel. My father, Anthony "Red" Brokaw, came from a family that owned a small railroad hotel. Both families worked tirelessly and made little money. Their values—honesty, fairness, diligence—sustained them.

Dad was a construction foreman for the Army Corps of Engineers. We moved several times during my childhood when he was assigned to a new project. He was a mechanical genius. If a machine had a motor, he could run it. If it was broken, he could fix it. On weekends he made extra money repairing cars and tractors. My mother, who worked as a post office clerk, was a bright woman who should have gone to college; it was simply out of reach economically. She was a voracious reader, a good writer, and the best editor I've ever had.

Mom was always interested in what was going on in the world. She and I would listen to the radio news every night (we didn't have a television until I was fifteen), hanging on Edward R. Morrow's every word. She loved politics, and she passed that passion along to me. The 1948 presidential election, in which Harry Truman upset Thomas Dewey, was a huge event in our house—we were dirt road Democrats and Harry Truman was one of us.

Dad's job allowed us to move into the middle class, but my parents took nothing for granted. When you live through something as devastating as the Depression, the memories of struggle remain fresh. But by the early fifties, America was overrun with optimism—the economy was booming and the future was filled with promise for families like ours. We settled in Yankton, South Dakota, with a population of nine thousand, the biggest town we'd ever lived in. The schools were excellent, and the community had a real core to it, imbued with those prairie-state values that did so much to shape me.

I thrived in Yankton. I was student body president, active on three sports teams, had the lead in the class plays, and was named governor of South Dakota American Legion Boys State. In that capacity, I visited New York City with the state's governor, where we made a joint television appearance. Accomplishments and awards came easily to me, and I began to take them for granted. One of my school friends later pulled me up short when he told me, "Tom, you rode that charm pony all over town."

I had a classmate in high school named Meredith Auld. Her father was a prominent doctor in Yankton. She graduated number two in our class, was class vice president, was an excellent musician, excelled at the University of South Dakota, and was even crowned Miss South Dakota.

Meredith and I were good friends; she was a cheerleader and I was a jock, and we shared a lot of laughs. She was everyone's picture of the ideal girl. But when it came to romance, she would have nothing to do with me. I had a bit of a reputation as a lady's man, and she told her friends, "I'm not going near that guy."

By the time I went off to the University of Iowa in Iowa City—the first person in my family to go to college—I was a whiz kid and everybody thought I was destined to accomplish world-changing deeds.

Then I crashed and burned.

I couldn't handle my newfound freedom at college. I rarely went to class, instead majoring in beer and girls. I once hitchhiked across the Midwest in the middle of the night, wound up in Minneapolis, and crashed on a friend's couch for five days. Of course my parents never knew.

Eventually I dropped out of school and got a menial job working in Sioux City, Iowa. I was surrounded by people who were struggling, many of them working two jobs and dealing with marital problems. I thought, "This is not the life that I want," and I moved back home, only to get a letter from Meredith. She let me know what she thought of me in pretty scathing terms. The letter was a real eye-opener for me. It was a friend doling out some very tough love.

I enrolled at the University of South Dakota in Vermillion, but I still wasn't ready to start behaving. Then I met Dr. William "Doc" Farber. Doc was a brilliant political scientist who had joined the faculty at USD in the middle of the Depression and been a mentor for generations of South Dakota kids. His ex-students included governors, senators, Rhodes Scholars, and successful businesspeople. His legacy is still growing: both of South Dakota's recent senators—Republican John Thune and Democrat Tim Johnson—are "Farber's boys."

Doc Farber stood about five feet four and carried a few extra pounds—he was a compact bundle of energy, exuding enthusiasm, encouragement, and curiosity. His passions were directed into the school and his students.

Shortly after I enrolled at USD, Farber invited me to dinner. We talked about the usual range of topics—books, politics, school. Then, over coffee and dessert, he said, "I have a plan for you. I want you to drop out and get the wine, women, and song out of your system. Come back when you can do us all some good." At first I was stunned, expecting, especially after such a nice dinner, that he would encourage and coddle me. Then I thought, "Geez, this is my ticket to party." I went home and told my parents Doc's advice. They weren't thrilled.

It wasn't what I had hoped. In the summer of 1960, I was twenty and living at home, working odd jobs, and feeling a little sorry for myself. The only thing that really excited me was the presidential election between Richard Nixon and John Kennedy, which Mom and I followed obsessively. Election Day was Tuesday, November 8, and I sat in front of the television in our living room from 7:00 p.m. until 8:00 a.m. on the morning of November 9, when Kennedy was finally declared the winner. That night changed my life—as I watched Chet Huntley and David Brinkley report on the seesawing vote totals, I said to myself, "*This* is what I want to do."

I got a job at a television station in Sioux City, Iowa, doing weather reports, station breaks, and the news, and I began to commute to the university, trying to patch up my erratic record. I would get up at 5:30 in the morning, get in the car at six, drive up to the university, go to class until noon, drive back to Sioux City, work until eleven at night, and get up and repeat it the next day. I worked six days a week and made $75.

Doc Farber helped me get through it by designing my curriculum to fit my schedule. He was leaning over my shoulder the entire time; he even set a minimum grade point average I had to attain. Farber ran a tough program; your final paper had to be master's degree quality. Mine was on Henry Kissinger, who was little known at that time. Because of my work schedule, I was late getting it finished, and I hoped Farber would give me a waiver so that I could graduate with my class of 1962. No chance. He said, "You owe me that paper. You don't get your degree until you finish it." So even though I had fulfilled all my other requirements, I didn't get my diploma until I finished that paper in 1964.

By not giving up on me, Farber changed my life. I heard from him almost every week until just before he died. We'd talk about what was going on in the news and how I was covering it. He could be complimentary, analytical, and critical, but always in a constructive way. Then he would say, "I've got a student who needs some help. How about a donation to the scholarship fund?" When he died in 2007, flags in South Dakota flew at half-mast for three days.

As I began to pull my life together, I reconnected with Meredith. She was changing, too. One of her early roommates was a young woman from South Texas named Carrie, who was something of a free spirit. She showed Meredith that college doesn't have to be only grade points and nights in the library. Earlier, Meredith had written me that dismissive letter, saying she didn't want to ever see me again, that my party boy behavior mystified my friends and saddened my parents. That letter was part of my wake-up call to change direction and once I reformed, Meredith had a change of heart, thank God.

We began to see each other and eighteen months later we were married, stunning her friends and mine.

Of all the lucky breaks in my life, that one is in a class of its own. For more than a half century I've been in awe of her intelligence and many skills—including becoming an expert horseback rider at age fifty. She has been a successful mother and grandmother, small business owner, corporate board member, philanthropist, environmentalist, skier, backpacker, and bridge player. Warren Buffett, a bridge enthusiast, likes to say, "I don't play for money, but if I did I'd want Meredith on my side."

I've had a life I could never have imagined when I was growing up in Yankton, South Dakota. I've been a witness to some of history's most important events and greatest tragedies. I've travelled the world and interviewed many of its leaders. The life I've had would not have happened without the generosity of spirit and unwavering support and honesty of Doc Farber, who came into my life and pushed and guided me when I needed it the most. He reinforced in me the prairie-state values of integrity, hard work, and caring for others that have guided me every step of the way. I owe so much of my life to Doc Farber's steadiness, and to my parents, and my wife of more than a half-century, Meredith.

BEN CARSON

Just how cool is neurosurgeon Ben Carson under pressure? Here's a famous story that sums it up: In 1987, Dr. Carson operated to separate the Binder twins, boys who were conjoined at the head. Time and Newsweek described it as the most complex surgery in history. The procedure called for cooling the patient's body to a point where the heart stopped, then pumping blood out and replacing it with a saline solution. It allowed surgeons to cut and repair blood vessels without the patient bleeding to death. When the surgery was complete, the surgical team warmed the patient's body, pumped the blood back in, and used a defibrillator to restart the heart. There was one important limitation: they had only one hour before the heart had to be restarted. They finished in just over fifty-nine minutes.

The turning points in Ben's life reminded me vividly of how powerful the role education can play in our lives, and at the same time, how important it is for young people to understand the value of a good education.

I'm from Detroit. My parents moved there from rural Tennessee. They'd gotten married when my father was twenty-eight and my mother was thirteen. She was one of twenty-four children. They were constantly shuffled from one home to another, never staying in the same place for long. My mother never got past the third grade.

In Detroit, they bought a house that was no more than one thousand square feet. It had a small yard, and my brother, Curtis, and I loved living there. Nothing about it felt small to us. We thought it was perfect.

But it wasn't. Curtis and I didn't know it, but my father was into drinking, drugs, and women. I suppose our mother had some sense of what he did and put up with it—until she discovered he was a bigamist. So when I was eight, my parents divorced. Mom got the house in the settlement, but she couldn't afford to live in it, so she rented it out, and she moved with Curtis and me to Boston, where we went to live with one of my aunts and her husband, my Uncle William.

I was impressed by what a hard worker my uncle was. But they didn't have much when we landed in the middle of their lives. They lived in a rat-, roach-, gang-, and wino-infested tenement and were surrounded by violence. Two of my older cousins, Beau and Louis Avery, were murdered there.

My mother had one goal: earn and save enough money to go back to Detroit. She worked two or three jobs at a time. She cleaned houses, one after another. It wasn't unusual for her to leave at 5:00 a.m. and come home after midnight.

Mom stood five feet three inches. She was pretty and had a steady stream of suitors, but she remained focused on Curtis and me, on finding ways for us to make our lives better than hers.

She was a person of faith, not just in God, but in the idea that the future could be better. She was never satisfied with our circumstances, and she believed that there was no reason to settle for what we had. I think some people found her odd. I found her wise.

She also was thrifty. I remember driving with her into the country on Sunday mornings. She would stop at a farmhouse, knock on the door, and ask if we could help with the harvest—usually picking corn or apples. The deal was, we could keep a quarter of what we picked. Usually, the farmers thought that was fair and so we'd get to work. Then we'd go home with our fresh produce, and Mom would can it.

My mother made a lot of our clothes. For Curtis and me, she used her imagination. Once she found a pair of jeans at the Goodwill store with a hole in one knee. She brought them home, sewed a patch over the hole, and put a matching patch on the other hole-free knee. When I wore them to school a lot of kids thought they looked cool and wanted to know where they could find jeans with similar patches.

We managed to move back to Detroit after a couple years. But we didn't get straight back into our old house because Mom still couldn't afford it. We lived in a crummy apartment in a horrible part of town. But we were on our own again. And eventually we got our house back.

School was a challenge for me. I was a terrible student. I thought I was stupid and so did everyone else. But Mom disagreed. She never believed I wasn't bright. She was an observant person who paid attention to how the world worked for people who were better off than we were.

For instance, she noticed that the wealthy people whose houses she cleaned spent more time reading and less time watching television than we did. So she came up with a plan that changed our lives. She put a strict limit on how much TV we could see. It was only two or three programs a week. My brother and I were not happy about that at all.

But there was an ancillary rule that we weren't happy with either: we had to read two books from the library every week and write reports on them. With only a third grade education, my mother had probably never written a book report in her life, but she understood the value of our doing so.

Something clicked for me. I'd always been amazed at how much the smarter kids seemed to know. No matter what a teacher asked, some kids always had the answer. I couldn't imagine or understand how they knew so much. But as I began to read more, I started finding that I sometimes raised my hand. It wasn't long before my mother didn't have to make me read anymore. In fact, I was more likely to hear a sharp "Benjamin, put down that book" when it was time for dinner.

I started with subjects that interested me. I loved animals, so I read books about animals. After I'd read every animal book for children in the Detroit Public Library, I switched to books about plants. And then rocks. I thought of rocks because we lived near some railroad tracks, which were lined with rocks, and I wanted to know more. I got to be quite an expert. I could look at a rock and tell you what type it was, where it had come from, and how it had formed.

This caught the attention of my fifth grade science teacher. He made me an assistant in the school's lab, where I helped take care of the animals and learned to use a microscope. That's when I discovered that a world of microorganisms could live in a single drop of pond water. I was on my way. Reading had made the difference.

That's not to say that the rest of my school days were easy. I had to survive all the usual trials of high school. Do I have the right friends? Am I wearing the right clothes? Do girls like me? Should I play basketball or study? And this was inner-city Detroit, so there were gangs—a lot of gangs. I tried to make friends with some of the gang leaders by helping them with their homework. It sometimes felt strange to realize that some of the toughest and most lethal guys in the neighborhood were worried about their homework, but they were. It was a symbiotic relationship. They got something they needed, and I got protection. Still, as I spent more and more time with these guys, my grades and attitude slipped.

I'd been complaining to Mom about not having the right clothes—the kind my new friends wore. She reminded me that everything we had, ate, and wore came from her work scrubbing floors, cleaning toilets, and doing all the dirty, menial jobs no one else wants to do. She then proposed an experiment. She'd give me all the money she earned that week. All I had to do was buy our food and pay our bills. After that, I could take any money that was left over and spend it on clothes.

Of course, as soon as I added everything up, I discovered that my mother was a financial genius. I stopped obsessing over clothes and gang-style posturing and put my head back into my books.

Looking back, I see how differently life turned out for some of the kids I wanted to emulate. There was one guy named Ezard. He was older because he'd flunked a couple of grades. He wore nice clothes and had a car and sometimes rode a motorcycle. He also had a .22-caliber pistol, a number of knives, and quite a following. When I went to my twenty-fifth class reunion, I realized all the cool guys were dead, including Ezard.

I just retired as director of pediatric neurosurgery at Johns Hopkins Hospital in Baltimore, Maryland. I had been director since I was thirty-three years old (I am now sixty-five) and over the course of my career, I've operated on 15,000 patients. I run into them regularly. And it's rewarding to see so many of them doing so well. Not long ago, I met a young man I'd operated on when he was nine months old. His parents had been told he had only a short time to live. He's twenty-one now.

In many ways, Detroit and the days I was afraid to raise my hand in class because I felt stupid seem like a long time ago. Back then, my mother, with her third-grade education, devoted herself to my brother and me, and she changed our lives. Throughout my career, every time I worked on a patient's brain, I thought of my mother and gave thanks for all the things she did for mine.

JAMES CARVILLE

I was among the many completely surprised when James Carville, advisor to Bill Clinton, married Republican consultant and campaign director for George H. W. Bush, Mary Matalin, in 1993, just months after the presidential election. How have they made it work for more than twenty years? "We just enjoy each other's company. Of course we have disagreements and issues, but all couples do. Our political differences can be aggravating, but we keep them in perspective. There are worse marital stresses than belonging to different political parties."

We often gravitate to heredity to understand and explain ourselves. In my conversations with James about the important moments in his life, I came to better understand how the environment— the community in which we grow up—joins forcibly with heredity to explain us and what we do with our lives.

The important thing to know about me is that I grew up in Carville, Louisiana. It's a small town that sits on a north-flowing bend of the Mississippi River, about sixteen miles south of Baton Rouge. Carville was home to Marine Hospital #66, which at the time was the world's largest treatment and research hospital for Hansen's disease, better known as leprosy.

As to why Carville is named Carville—it wasn't for a noble reason such as my great granddaddy being an important figure in Louisiana history. Carville used to be called Island (although it is not, in fact, an island), but there were other Islands nearby, including Sicily Island and Pecan Island. The mail kept getting sent to the wrong Island, so the post office decided to change the town's name. My grandfather was the postmaster at the time and, in a burst of familial pride, picked the new name. On June 9, 1909, Island became Carville.

I came into the world in 1944, the first of my parents' eight children. This was pretty much the average size of a Catholic family in Louisiana in the 1940s. I spent my remarkably happy childhood between two homes—mine and my grandparents'. When I wanted a change of scene, I'd get on my horse and ride the mile and a half between the two. Compared to most people in Carville, we were affluent—our house had three bedrooms and we had a car. My dad, Chester, owned the general store and, like his dad, he was also the postmaster.

Dad's store had been started by my great-grandmother. It sold just about everything—shoes, sandwiches, nails, canned corn, aspirin, beer, tools. Then a new road was built, which made it much easier for folks to get to the big supermarkets that were opening around Baton Rouge. Even as a boy it was clear to me that the stock-everything country store was not long for this world. I advised my father to scale down his inventory, but he felt an obligation to serve the community and resisted change. I watched him ride the business into the sunset, worrying himself sick. He died young of a heart attack. The lesson I took from the store's slow death was to take aggressive action when situations turn south. Sometimes I'm too quick to pull the plug, but, on the whole, the strategy has worked for me.

Carville was probably 85 percent African American. I hung out and played with black kids all my life. In fact, I tended to identify with the African Americans in town. That's why I became a Democrat. I said to anyone who would listen, "These people are getting a bad deal here. They work hard, are great neighbors, and they don't have the same rights that we do." Not everyone appreciated that sentiment.

I learned my sympathies at home. My mother, Lucille, taught us to respect everyone equally. She was a formidable woman with a much stronger personality than my father. She had a great nickname: Miz Nippy. During the Depression, down-and-out men would travel all over rural America, hopping freight trains, sleeping and scrounging food wherever they could. There was one fellow named Nip who lived in the woods behind nearby Avoyelles Parish for a while. Mama would take him food—and folks just started calling her Miz Nippy. Some people are named after royalty, others after sports heroes or movie stars. I've always taken great pride in the fact that my Mama was named after a hobo.

She was also one of the greatest salespeople I've ever known. With the store struggling, she went to work selling *World Book Encyclopedia* sets door-to-door everywhere she could, and she often took me along as her helper.

"Now, James, look for a bicycle and a bass boat," she'd say as we drove past modest homes in the various neighborhoods.

"How come?"

"The bicycle means that the family has kids. The boat means they have enough money to buy a boat."

When we spotted a bike and a boat we'd park, walk up the front steps, knock, and wait for the lady of the house to answer. She would invite us in, we'd sit in the living room, and after some pleasantries Mama would turn to me and ask, "James, what's the capital of Vermont?"

"Montpelier," I would dutifully answer.

"When was the French Revolution?"

"1789 to 1799."

Mama would then credit my vast knowledge to the *World Book Encyclopedia*. The lady of the house would consider this and then say, "I have to ask my husband."

The husband would appear, and Mama would make her pitch. He would listen before saying, "Mrs. Carville, I appreciate your time, and

I'm sure you're right about the encyclopedia, but right now we've got bills to pay. Why don't you come back at another time, and we'll be glad to talk about it."

"You know, sir, I couldn't help but notice that you have a bass boat."

"I do indeed," the husband would say proudly, not realizing he just stepped right into Mama's trap.

"So you're putting off buying educational materials for your children, and yet you indulge yourself with a bass boat?"

Sale made.

Mama taught me there's honor in being a good salesperson, especially when you're selling a worthy product. Politics is all about selling.

Marine Hospital #66, which took care of those with leprosy, was the best place to work in the parish and many of Carville's blacks had decent jobs there, government jobs that came with health care and a pension. There was less discrimination at Marine Hospital than at a lot of other places in Louisiana, and the jobs—which were often passed down from parents to children—carried some prestige.

The hospital attracted researchers and doctors from all over the world, some of whom stayed for months and even years. I got to meet them and hang out with their kids, who filled my head with stories of exotic places. I developed tremendous curiosity. A lot of rural folks never venture far from home. Thanks to my exposure to Marine Hospital #66 I became aware of—and eager to explore—the wider world.

An interest in politics ran in my family. My grandfather was on the commission that ran the parish. Dad would read the newspaper out loud and insert editorial comments along the lines of, "I can't believe what those jackasses are up to now." I had my first political job when I was in high school, working for a guy who was running for the state legislature. I went around town putting up his signs and tearing down the other guy's.

During high school I had a summer job at a bank in Baton Rouge. I ran a lot of errands, and some of them took me to the state capitol building. I would watch the legislature in session. Louisiana has a long history of producing colorful and sometimes crooked politicians, and I found the whole thing riveting.

After I got my law degree in 1973, I went to work at a law firm in Baton Rouge. I was there for six years, but I didn't like being a lawyer. It was boring, and I was restless. I was afraid I'd spend the rest of my life behind a desk. Then a friend ran for mayor of Baton Rouge, and I worked as a consultant to his campaign. I was jumping out of bed every morning, full of fight and energy. We won, and I was hooked.

I feel very fortunate these days. We live in New Orleans, about seventy miles downriver from Carville. I'm near my roots, and they sustain me. My dad ignited my curiosity about the larger world. His commitment to his store as a community resource made me proud, and his inability to adapt to change made me aggressive in responding to it. My Mama's skill at selling encyclopedias helped me understand the need to get inside people's heads. Having Marine Hospital #66 in Carville broadened my thinking and made me more compassionate. Growing up with African Americans helped me understand struggle and want to fight for the underdog. Carville might be a speck of a town, but its riverbed soil is very deep and rich.

DEBBI FIELDS

If you ask famed entrepreneur Debbi Fields for the secret to her success, she'll happily share this story of her very first day in the cookie business. All alone, Fields opened her first store in the international food court of her local mall. She couldn't sleep the night before, and arrived before dawn to start baking. At 9:00 a.m., she opened up the doors and waited for the customers to pour in. As lunchtime approached, she had not sold a single cookie. Then it hit her: Why not give them away? So she put the cookies on a baking sheet and headed out into the mall. She stopped people and invited them to have a taste. She made $75 in sales that day and in the weeks and months that followed, she realized that free samples were her best advertising. The more cookies she gave away, the more she sold.

Debbi shared with me a valuable lesson she learned from the defining moments in her life: there's nothing complex or magical at the root of a success. It's not always a secret formula found in some business book. Sometimes our best path, either in life or business, is to find what we do well and then do it to the best of our ability.

I can still remember my first batch. I was about eleven years old. I got a bowl and mixed up the available ingredients—white flour, margarine, imitation chocolate chips, and imitation vanilla. I shaped them into little mounds on a baking sheet, put them in the oven, and within minutes their wonderful aroma enveloped me. I removed them from the oven when they were nicely browned, took a bite, and thought, "This is the best thing I have ever tasted." From then on, my personal food pyramid was comprised completely of cookies.

I started to bake cookies all the time, and I carried them with me in my bag, sharing them with family and friends. Watching people break into a smile when they bit into one became very important to me. Not only did it extend the hand of friendship, build a bridge, and make me feel good, but it also gave me something I needed more of, which was validation.

I got my first job when I was thirteen, as a ball girl for the Oakland As. I stood behind the third-base line and retrieved foul balls. With my first paycheck, I headed straight to the supermarket and bought butter, real chocolate, and real vanilla. I rushed home and made a fresh batch of cookies. The first taste literally changed my life. I'd discovered the joys of butter—and I made the decision then and there that I was never going to make another chocolate chip cookie without using the best ingredients.

It never crossed my mind to turn my cookies into a career. No one in my family had gone to college. My father was a welder. You were supposed to go to high school, then get married and find a decent salaried job.

My main obstacle early in life was confidence. Growing up, I struggled with my sense of self and where I fit in the world. I didn't have a lot of girlfriends or boyfriends. I was focused on my big sisters, on getting their attention and approval. I always wanted to tag along with them, to fit in. They started calling me "Hey, stupid." That was my nickname. It hurt; it made me feel like I didn't measure up. I became something of a loner, working as hard as I could at school and after-school jobs. I wanted to prove to my sisters, to the world, and to myself that I could succeed. Ironically, their belittling nickname made me work harder.

I enrolled in a junior college. It was at this time that I met Randy Fields, my future husband and business partner. Randy was in sales, and he was smart, handsome, and charismatic. He had gone to Stanford, and I was slightly intimidated by his education and the world he lived in, which was much more privileged than my background. People gravitated to Randy; at social gatherings, I was almost an afterthought. Someone would come up to me and ask, "And what do you do?" When I told them I was a homemaker, I could see them just write me off. I was young and blonde, and people stereotyped me, and assumed that I had nothing upstairs.

It all came to a head one night. We were at the house of a man who was a potential client of Randy's. The place was palatial, and I was in the library with our host, just the two of us. I was all of twenty years old and nervous; all I cared about was saying the right thing and making a good impression. We were talking, and he asked me, "Debbi, what are you going to do with your life?" I answered, "I'm just trying to get orientated." He looked at me for a moment, then strode over to a bookshelf and grabbed a thick, leather-bound volume. As he got closer I could read the title: *Webster's Dictionary*. He dropped the book in my hands and said, "If you can't speak the English language, then don't speak at all. The word is not 'orientated,' it's 'oriented.'" Then he walked out of the room.

I sat there angry, humiliated, and at a loss. I was certain that I'd hurt Randy's chances of getting hired and I felt momentarily defeated. Then I had an epiphany and told myself, "I'm going to show this man." It was a devastating evening, but it changed my life.

Of course, the next morning I still had to face the question I had been asked the night before: What am I going to do with my life?

I was sitting at my kitchen table when I remembered something my father used to say to me: "Debbi, true fulfillment is when you love what you do." He loved his work and wanted nothing more than to be the world's best welder. He wasn't motivated by money; he was motivated by pride. I thought, "I'm really good at making cookies." That was it. I was going into the cookie business.

Maybe it was the first sign of confidence or simply the acknowledgement that I didn't have anything to lose, but I felt I could do this. I had no experience running a business, but I could rely on what I knew, the basics—the best ingredients, the best recipe, the best cookie. And I knew my customer because, in many ways, I was that customer.

Then I had to raise capital. I wrote my first business plan and visited any number of bankers; I'd been advised not to bring the cookies and to dress conservatively. As a twenty-year-old woman without an MBA, I knew the odds were not in my favor, so I decided to do just the opposite: be myself and dress in brightly colored clothes, armed with a platter of cookies.

In spite of my passion and good intentions, I got a lot of no's. These were very conservative bankers, and they just couldn't see a profit in me. It was disheartening, and I was tempted to throw in the towel numerous times. But the easiest thing for any of us to do is to give up and I didn't want to be a quitter. This was my life, and I was going to make something of it, no matter how many men in dark suits gave me the thumbs-down.

My mantra became "no is an unacceptable answer." I became even more passionate in my presentation, and I found a man who said yes. When you're asking for money, the most important thing isn't a business plan or the clothes you wear or even your amazing cookies. What matters most is making people believe in you, believe that you will find a way to succeed, no matter how many setbacks you endure.

This might sound like a rather simple life lesson, but you have to persevere even when everything is stacked against you. I kept getting knocked down, but I learned how to get back up. That is the hard part: actually getting back up. But, the world is out there for the taking. My advice: find your own cookie, the thing that inspires you and gives you much-needed confidence in yourself. Then go out and share it with the world. It worked for me.

ROBERT GATES

Among my favorite stories is the one about Bob Gates becoming the first secretary of defense to take his motorcade through a Burger King. After giving the commencement address at the Virginia Military Institute, the secretary was headed back to the airport in Lexington, Virginia. It was lunchtime and Gates said, "I'm hungry, let's go to the Burger King." So he took the entire motorcade, state police and all, through the drive-thru. The employees were a little surprised—in rural southwest Virginia, the employees of Burger King don't see that many customers at one time in uniforms, dark suits, and sunglasses.

Abraham Lincoln once said, "I don't think much of a man who is not wiser today than he was yesterday." Bob shows us that everything we need to learn in life is available—in the examples of others. When we take time to identify and reflect on the people and things we admire, we have the unique and rewarding opportunity to enrich not only our lives but the lives of everyone around us.

I learned countless lessons from the men and women of the CIA and the armed forces who continue to serve this nation on a daily basis. Their lessons were profound and everlasting. But it was the personal influences early in my life and the examples of those I came to admire that gave me the strength and wisdom to serve them better.

I was born in Wichita, Kansas, in 1943. My father, Melville, was a wholesale auto-parts salesman. My mother, Isabel, was a homemaker.

I have a brother, Jim, who is almost eight years older than me. Because of our age difference, I grew up in awe of my brother, complete with little-sibling rivalry.

As "Andy Griffith and Mayberry" as it sounds, my childhood was about as idyllic as could be. Life revolved around family, school, church, and the Boy Scouts. My parents were honorable people with strong views about character. They had no patience for lying, hypocrisy, unethical behavior, shirking responsibility, or putting on airs. They made it clear to me that I was as good as anybody else. They also made it clear that I was no better than anybody else. Those were not just words to my parents.

My father was an avid golfer, and we belonged to a country club, mostly so he could play golf. He was a member for almost thirty years and he loved the club, its members, and the close friendships he had made over the years. But at some point, the membership and club started to change. New members joined, not to play golf or contribute to the overall well-being of the club, but to improve their own social standing and to make business connections that were otherwise difficult to make. When the new members wanted more for themselves, they convinced the majority of the membership to move the club to a better part of town. Disappointed in the new direction the club was taking and unable to stop the move, my parents quit the club.

A similar situation arose at our church, Disciples of Christ Church, which my parents had been attending for decades. The neighborhood around the church was declining economically and becoming more diverse racially and ethnically. The church elders decided to build a new church in a more affluent neighborhood. My parents disagreed with the decision, feeling the church should stay put and work to help the neighborhood. And so when the church moved, my parents left the congregation.

I had a lot of freedom as a kid. Wichita was a safe place to grow up, and, while my parents had certain rules, my brother and I were allowed to explore and roam.

I was devoted to Boy Scouts. The values I learned scouting are with me to this day. My brother and I are both Eagle Scouts, and after I served as secretary of defense, I became president of the Boy Scouts of America. It was a family tradition—I have a picture in my office of my father in a Boy Scout uniform, taken in 1918.

I half-jokingly say that the only management course I ever took was the National Junior Leader Training Program at the Philmont Scout Ranch when I was fourteen years old. The ranch is in the mountains outside of Raton, New Mexico. I was named a patrol leader, which meant I was in charge of eight boys my age or younger. I would assign duties such as meal prep, cleanup, or striking the tents. I learned how to get people to take on tasks they hadn't realized they wanted to. That skill came in handy in Washington.

I went to William & Mary as a premed student, an aspiration derailed my first semester by a D in calculus. I changed my major to history. William & Mary is in Williamsburg, Virginia, which was founded in 1632, and just being around all that colonial history was inspiring. From there, I moved steadily eastward—my undergraduate degree was in European history, my master's was in Eastern European history, and my doctorate was in Russian and Soviet history.

I was already at the Central Intelligence Agency when I earned my PhD. My dissertation was titled "Soviet Sinology: An Untapped Source for Kremlin Views and Disputes Relating to Contemporary Events in China."

When I was up for confirmation as deputy director of the CIA in 1982, a friend at the Georgetown Library called to tell me that a handful of journalists were at the library reading my dissertation. My reaction: "It serves them right."

I've had many mentors during my career. I always tell young people to connect with people a few rungs up from them, whose behavior they respect, and reach out to them for advice and guidance. It's all about learning.

Sometimes I learned what lessons not to do, which can be just as valuable. Stansfield Turner was a four-star admiral in the US Navy when he was named to head the CIA, and he brought sixty navy people with him to the agency. It had a tremendous negative impact because it sent a message that he didn't trust the people already in place. It amounted to a hostile takeover.

Turner's example was on my mind on December 18, 2006, when I walked into the Pentagon—alone. I didn't even bring an assistant with me. The message I wanted to send: I trust you, and the last thing we need in the middle of two wars is a neophyte secretary of defense surrounded by neophyte staffers.

I think one thing that helped me navigate the treacherous waters of Washington was that people knew that I was willing to walk away, that it wasn't about ego for me. And when I was ready, I left. I had been secretary of defense for four and a half years, and we had been at war every day during that time.

In walking away from power, my inspiration was George Washington. When I give talks about the recent revolutions in the Arab world, I point to the history of revolution going back 250 years—the American, the French, the Russian, the Chinese, the Iranian, and a host of others. Of all of those, there is only one that turned out reasonably well in the first decades after its conclusion, and that was our own. And it was because George Washington was willing to walk away from power.

Looking back, I realize how my life has been so firmly directed by the precious lesson taught to me by my parents and mentors about trusting one's inner compass, that small but persistent voice that tells us what is right and wrong. My parents could have easily stayed with the members of their country club and church as they both moved to economically richer and less racially divided neighborhoods, but they trusted themselves and their values. They showed me what it is to have real, everyday courage. Likewise, George Washington could have grasped onto power, causing untold damage to our newly formed republic. But he didn't—he walked away.

What I have learned from this simple and rather uncomplicated life of mine is this: nothing can make a greater difference in the quality of life than the insight and moral compass we capture from the examples of others. We just need to pay attention to the details.

BARRY GIBBONS

In 1988, Barry Gibbons was offered the job as head of Burger King. It wasn't going to be an easy job. Operations were stale and bloated. There were thirteen layers of management. Spending was out of control as evidenced by the $50,000 allowance each executive had for office furnishings. When asked about the challenge he faced, he likes to tell this story. Upon his arrival, the company sent a limousine to ferry him from the Miami airport to the airport-adjacent hotel, a two-minute walk. Barry's first response to the waste, "I could have gotten in the front door of the limo, crawled out the back, and practically been at the hotel." Thus began the era of transformation at Burger King that would culminate with Gibbons on the cover of Fortune magazine under the headline, "The Turnaround King."

There's a powerful lesson in the defining moment that Barry shared with me and that is: mistakes are better made when you are young. This is such an important message to today's young people— and to the parents and teachers who hope to guide them. We all make mistakes growing up; the question is, are we willing to take them seriously and learn from them?

When I was sixteen, I got a major kick in the shins that put me on a bad path in life.

I was born in Manchester, England, in 1946, the year after World War II ended. The whole country was giddy with peace—except perhaps for my father, Ernest. He'd been an officer in the British Army, stationed first in India and then Singapore. He was captured when Singapore fell to the Japanese on February 15, 1942. The experience stiffened an already stiff fellow. Dad's idea of dressing down was to wear a cravat instead of necktie. I was always a pretty relaxed sort, even as a toddler. My wife, Judy, says my approach to the world is crumpled.

My father and I were very different, and there was a fair amount of head butting between us during my childhood. When I was a teenager in the sixties, the generation gap became a chasm. My father was "God Save the Queen," I was "A Hard Day's Night." He was an ex-soldier, I was a James Dean wannabe, but, in this instance, a rebel without a clue.

My homework was never done on time. I skipped school. I was insolent. Those were the days of corporal punishment so my backside was quite frequently caned, and it seemed as if I spent more time in detention than in the classroom.

Somehow I made it through to my last year of preparatory-purgatory school. I had three weeks to go before I would take my university entry exams. That's when "the incident" happened. It was in history class. We had finished the syllabus and were using those last weeks to prepare for the exam. One day the teacher informed us that three days hence we would be answering an essay question on the causes of the First World War. I actually went home and prepared. When the day arrived the teacher announced, "Change of plan. You are going to answer a question on Bismarck's foreign policy from 1870 on."

The classroom fell silent. We had prepared for one essay question and now had to answer an altogether different one. Our teacher explained that, during the actual exam, we would not know the questions in advance. This perfectly reasonable explanation did not penetrate my thick head.

I was angry, and from my desk at the back of the classroom, I expressed my displeasure with great vehemence. I don't recall my exact words, but I'm sure they were colorful and to the point. The teacher ejected me from the class. As I was walking to the front of the classroom, he glared at me. I gave him a shove in the chest.

Not a smart move. I was marched to the headmaster's office and was sent home. My father, who had been phoned by the school, was waiting. The verdict was stark: I was expelled. I would be allowed back on the premises to take my exams, but I would get no reference. That was the sting in the tail because, in England, I needed a proper reference to get a job or into a university.

When the implications of my idiocy sunk it, I got surly and depressed. I basically sat around the house for the next three years, which gave me plenty of time to reflect on my lot.

I had been tolerated at school and at home when I was playing the rebel. The minute I actually rebelled, they swatted me down. I realized that there are some forces in life that you can't beat. It's like trying to defy gravity.

When I turned eighteen, I got a job as a laborer in a brewery. They hired me because I was young and fit. Meanwhile, my friends were starting careers or going to university. Still, I was happy with my job. My father was mortified—he didn't raise his son to work as a laborer.

Two lucky occurrences got me on track. I was on a soccer team. There was a small convenience shop next to the stadium where we played, and I got to be friendly with the owner. The shop was a sideline for him; he was a manager at Shell. One day he told me about a job opening there. "It's a fancy clerk's job," he said. "I'll put a good word in for you."

I applied for the job—the first and only job I've ever applied for. I got it. It was dull. Shell was kind enough to give me a day off every week to go to college and perhaps rescue my academic career. During this period, I moved from Manchester to Liverpool and audited a business class at Liverpool University. I can't say I was a good student. In fact, I can state with certainty that I was a bad one. I missed classes and did shoddy work, but I did like provoking and participating in classroom debates. I loved thrashing out business decisions, albeit hypothetical ones.

One day the professor asked me to stay after class for a chat. My heart sank, because any time in my life that I'd received a summons like that, it spelled trouble. After the other students had filed out of the classroom, there was a long silence and then the professor said, "You should be up here lecturing to these students, not playing the fool. If you start working seriously in this class, I'll get you into Liverpool University as a mature student." It was an astonishing moment. For once I had nothing to say.

When I was sixteen years old I made a big mistake, and I paid for it. I have spent a lifetime thinking, reflecting, and using the lessons from it. The way I look at it, I was damned lucky it happened early.

RUDY GIULIANI

I often play golf with football coaching great Lou Holtz and former New York City mayor Rudy Giuliani, but rarely do I play with them together. The banter between the two of them makes it too difficult for me to concentrate on the game. For example, we were playing together at Old Collier Golf Club in Naples, Florida. This one morning, Rudy was not playing particularly well and the more frustrated he became, the worse he played. After one especially bad shot, Lou walked over to Rudy, who was rather dejected.

"Your son Andrew, he is a great golfer isn't he?"

Taking the bait, Rudy's face lit up with pride and said, "Well, yes he is, Lou."

"Normally," Lou said with his typical quick wit, "doesn't a son learn to play good golf from his father?"

Everyone laughed, especially Rudy.

Rudy has always inspired me, in part because I found his life to be an expression of faith. It is true that to most people he is thought of as a man of action, often defined by what he has done. But the influences in his life that Rudy shared with me showed something different: that no matter who we are or how strong and decisive we seem to be, many of us still look for spiritual guidance in difficult times.

I was born and spent my first seven years in Flatbush, a working-class, Italian American neighborhood of Brooklyn, New York. One rainy day when I was five, my mother went to the bank, leaving me with my grandmother. When she got home, she realized the teller had given her an extra hundred dollars. She said, "I'm going to have to go back." My grandmother said, "Oh, come on, you can at least wait until it stops raining." My mother said, "No, I've got to go right away because the teller will be in torture until I get back."

She headed toward the door, then turned around, came back, and took my hand, saying, "You're coming with me." My grandmother said, "What, you're going to take him out in the rain?" Mom said, "This is an important lesson." So we walked to the bank in the rain. Mom had to lift me up to see the teller, who was a middle-aged woman. She returned the extra money. The teller closed the window and came out to see us, in tears. "Thank you so much for doing this," she said, "because this would have been the third time my drawer was short, and I would probably have gotten fired."

The importance of honesty and integrity was drilled into me during my childhood. I think one reason was because my father had gotten into serious trouble as a young man, and he ended up going to jail.

Dad was pretty tough. He was nearsighted and was fitted for glasses when he was five years old. That was the cue for the neighborhood bullies, who called him names and beat him up. My grandfather's brother knew someone who ran a gym, and he took Dad over there—he must have been the youngest would-be boxer they'd ever seen. But the sport toughened him up, and he later had a short career as a professional boxer. Then he got into trouble. When he got out of jail he opened a bar and grill, which is what he was doing when I was born.

During my childhood and all through high school, I often wanted to be a priest. Mom and Dad encouraged me. I think they suspected I wouldn't go through with it, but felt that the training and discipline would be good for me. At other times I wanted to be a doctor, a base-ball player, and a pilot. But priest was number one. I didn't even apply to college. When I graduated from high school I was headed for the Montfort Fathers Seminary in Bay Shore, Long Island; their purpose was to train missionary priests for work in Africa and Haiti. I had been accepted. My high school yearbook was full of notes wishing me luck in the seminary.

I graduated in June, seminary started in September, so I decided to relax a little bit more than usual. One day some friends and I went to Jones Beach. I met a girl. The hit song that summer was "Itsy-Bitsy, Teenie-Weenie Yellow Polka-Dot Bikini." Well, this girl was wearing an itsy-bitsy, teenie-weenie yellow polka-dot bikini. Let's just say it made a strong impression on me.

For the next two weeks, I was obsessed and conflicted. I thought about going to the seminary, how wonderful it would be to study theology, going to Haiti or Africa to help people. And then there was that bikini.

So I went to the seminary and talked to the priest in charge. I explained my dilemma. He laughed and said, "This is quite natural. You shouldn't join now because you're not ready. Take two years off, go to work or go to college, and if you decide you want to become a priest after all, come back and see me."

I went home and told my parents, wondering if they were going to be disappointed. But, as I suspected, they saw it coming. So now I had to get into college. The Christian Brothers also ran Manhattan College (which is actually in the Bronx), and so I was able to get in at the last minute. I began in the premed program, thinking that as a doctor I could still go to Africa and save people—but I could bring my wife along.

It turned out that I didn't like premed. Then I thought about joining the air force because I wanted to fly. So I joined ROTC but had to drop out of flight training because I had punctured eardrums. Then I started to think I would become a teacher. Then I changed my mind again. I had a Methodist girlfriend at the time, and I spoke to her minister about becoming a Methodist minister. He suggested

Episcopalian would be an easier transition because the theology and ceremonies are similar to Catholicism. I told my dad this. He was the most religious member of the family and wasn't wild about the idea: "You're crazy, you're really nuts. Will you get this priest thing out of your head! First of all, Episcopalian priests don't have Italian names. You want to be a priest, be a real priest."

I was in my senior year of college, and I didn't know what I was going to do. I had a psychology professor who was also my guidance counselor, Jerry Cashman. Jerry said, "I think you should take an aptitude test. It reveals what you're naturally good at. Find that and you'll have a happy life." So I took a four-hour test, and the results came back a couple of months later saying I'd be a good lawyer.

So I became a lawyer.

For the next twenty-five years, my religious thinking was not far from me. But after being elected mayor of New York, it came back in a big way when I met Father Mychal Judge, the chaplain of the New York City Fire Department and a man who became my spiritual advisor. Judge was a Franciscan priest and a charismatic figure. Six feet tall and movie star handsome, he'd had his personal struggles—he was a recovering alcoholic—but that only strengthened his faith and empathy. He was a legend in the fire department for his courage and devotion. He visited every hospitalized firefighter daily, and he called widows and widowers for years after a death. At the same time, he loved nothing more than to join a fire drill and chop down a door with an axe.

Our friendship deepened with each passing year. When I was in trouble, particularly when my second marriage fell apart in a very public way, I'd come home to Gracie Mansion at night and there would be a note from Father Judge. In it he would tell me he knew things were rough, and he'd even tell me when he felt I'd done something wrong. I'd read the note and cry. He didn't give me unconditional support, but he let me know that life is complicated and that you can make up for your misdeeds by doing good deeds. He would remind me that Jesus noted the good deeds—caring for the sick, helping the poor, protecting the weak—as well as our sins and failures.

On the morning of September 11, 2001, I was having breakfast at the Peninsula Hotel when an aide brought me word that a plane had hit the World Trade Center. I raced downtown. By the time I arrived, both towers had been hit.

As I was walking toward the fire department command post, I saw Father Judge walking in the other direction. He always had a smile on his face but he now looked serious. I called out to him, took his hand, and asked if he would say a prayer. "We should all pray," he said.

That was the last time I saw Father Judge. He was inside the North Tower, in the lobby, helping the firefighters, when the South Tower collapsed. The force of the blast blew him across the lobby, and he was fatally injured. He was the first recorded death that morning.

I didn't find out about Father Judge's death right away. After being trapped for a short while in a building across from the Trade Center, I moved to a command post at police headquarters across town. I knew I had to make what would be the most important statement of my life. I thought of Father Judge and wanted him by my side. Then an aide told me that he had been killed. I didn't have a moment to grieve, but I remember thinking, "I'm really on my own now."

In the difficult days that followed, Father Judge's faith and humanity filled my heart and guided my actions. It's been said that I did a good job in the aftermath of that terrible day. If that's so, all the credit goes to Father Judge.

It has been an amazing and, in many ways, heartening journey. While I long ago gave up the idea of being a priest, my parents were right. The priesthood would give me the training and discipline that I would ultimately need to live my life.

SAL GIUNTA

Like so many seniors in high school, Sal Giunta was undecided about his future. He was working part-time in a Subway shop when a US Army recruiting commercial came on the radio promising a free T-shirt to anyone who met with the recruiter. He thought, "That's cool, I can always use a free T-shirt." So he met with the recruiter, who explained that the country was engaged in two wars, in Afghanistan and Iraq, and that the nation needed him. Giunta said, "Thanks for the pep talk, but I came here for the T-shirt."

We think we know ourselves pretty well, who and what we are. But do we? Is there a test, a turning point so powerful, that not until we experience it will we really know?

The moon was full the night of October 25, 2007, illuminating the rocky ridge, where our team of eight, part of a platoon of eighteen men, stood watch. Stands of pines dotted the ridge. Below us was Afghanistan's Korengal Valley, which we called the Valley of Death. Our mission was to watch over fellow soldiers who were in one of the valley's villages. They were negotiating with elders for intelligence about a recent Taliban attack that had killed an American soldier.

We'd been out for four days, sleeping on the ground. Not that we slept much. On our fourth day, we received orders to return to Korengal Outpost, the farm in the valley that had been turned into a rudimentary base. We were all looking forward to taking off our boots for the first time in ninety-six hours.

We began the hike back. The moon was so bright we didn't need our night-vision goggles. We walked single file with about thirty to forty-five feet between us. We stayed apart to minimize injuries or casualties if we were hit by a grenade or rocket.

We'd been hiking for about fifteen minutes when a burst of bullets and grenades exploded around us. It sounded like fireworks—screaming, booming, whizzing, cracking. There were more bullets in the air than stars in the sky. My best friend Josh Brennan was hit. Specialist Frank Eckrode was hit. I returned fire and advanced.

Two of my men, Privates First Class Kaleb Casey and Garret Clary, were also firing back. Casey stood up to shoot his weapon, the M249, which can shoot one hundred rounds a minute, making himself a target. It gave me cover and I pushed forward to our squad leader, Sergeant Erick Gallardo. A bullet hit his helmet, and he collapsed. I thought he'd been severely injured or killed. As I grabbed his body armor to pull him to cover, I was hit in the chest, but my body armor deflected the bullet. Then Gallardo stumbled to his feet, stunned but alive. We both began throwing grenades. We were so close to the enemy that our grenades landed behind them, protecting us from the explosion.

As I threw my last grenade, Gallardo and I came up to Eckrode, on the ground. He had been shot twice in his leg and twice in his chest. While Gallardo assessed his condition, I kept firing and advancing.

I came to a clearing among the pines and saw two Taliban dragging a man away by his hands and feet. I was probably fifteen meters away, running at a dead sprint, before I realized that the man they were dragging was an American soldier. I fatally shot one of the Taliban and wounded the other, who raced down the side of the ridge.

When I reached the American soldier, I discovered that it was my friend Brennan. He was badly hurt. We were in a no-man's-land, which meant that we could get shot by friend or foe. I grabbed Brennan by the handle on his vest and ran toward our line.

I got Brennan out of the line of fire and called for our medic, Hugo Mendoza. There was no response. I found out later that he'd been killed in the first couple seconds of the ambush. I assessed Brennan. He was shot in his arms, legs, and chest. He had taken shrapnel to his face, and his bottom jaw was mostly gone. I tried to keep his airway open to reduce the bleeding. By this time, reinforcements had arrived and a nurse performed a tracheotomy. At one point, Brennan stopped breathing. I pumped the bag to force air into his lungs.

"Morphine," Brennan mumbled.

"You'll get out and tell your hero stories," I said.

"I will, I will . . ."

The shooting diminished. The enemy's firepower was depleted, and they began to retreat. We used our ponchos as makeshift stretchers for the dead and wounded. A helicopter appeared above us, and we hoisted Brennan, Mendoza, Eckrode, and two other men out. We divvied up their gear and equipment and began the two-hour hike to base. When we got back, we found out that Mendoza and Brennan had died.

Only a couple of days after the ambush, my superiors told me they were going to recommend me for a commendation. I was furious. I had just lost my best friend and Mendoza. The idea of exploiting the tragedy of their deaths with some heroic storyline sickened me. What was the point? It wouldn't bring them back. Besides, I was only a soldier doing what I was trained to do, like thousands of others who serve their nation.

There was nothing heroic about how I had gotten here. I just wanted a T-shirt. But after I left the recruiting station, I started thinking about serving. It could be an adventure. I could spit and swear and shoot guns and see the world. And I liked the idea of helping to win the wars we were in.

I enlisted in November 2003. I joined the airborne infantry, mainly because jumping out of a plane added an extra $150 to my monthly check. After training at Fort Benning, Georgia, I was assigned to the

173rd Airborne Brigade in Vicenza, Italy. I went on my first combat tour in Afghanistan in March 2005.

Afghanistan, especially when you get out of the cities, is a primitive country. My unit was housed in farmers' mud huts in a valley in the southeast part of the country, at least forty kilometers from any other Americans. The valley was studded with almond and apricot orchards, as well as fields of marijuana and poppies. The poppies were used to make heroin, but the drugs weren't our concern. The Taliban were.

Our platoon was all guys; at that time, the infantry didn't accept women. The average age was about twenty, and we were from all over the country—whites, blacks, Latinos, and mixed race. At first, we only had one thing in common: we were always hungry.

Just two months after my deployment, the reality of war first hit home. Our thirty-five-man platoon had been in a number of gunfights but had never been hit by any improvised explosive devices (IEDs). Then one of our trucks ran over one, killing three men and blowing the legs off another. We lost a fifth man later that week in a raid on a Taliban leader's compound. We took the target out but one of our guys was killed.

Until then, I thought that you go to war, kill the bad guys, come home, drink beer, kiss pretty ladies, and you're a hero. That week reset everything. It's one thing to look into a casket and see a lifeless body in a suit; it's another to see a body blown up in front of you. I felt overwhelmed. These were young, able-bodied men in the prime of their lives. Their deaths made me question not only why we were in Afghanistan, but war in general and my own future. I was scared for my life.

After the attack near Korengal Valley and Mendoza's and Brennan's deaths, I was put on rear detachment. My job was to support the families of the men of the 173rd Brigade who were in war zones. I was in charge of forty-three wives and sixty-four children who were living at the base, acting as middleman in their dealings with the military, the Italian government, and other authorities.

On September 9, 2010, I was sitting at my desk when the phone rang. Since most of my work was conducted by e-mail, this was a relatively rare occurrence. I answered, and the person on the line identified himself as a colonel at the Pentagon. He confirmed my name and Social Security number and then said, "You'll be getting a call at this time tomorrow from the White House. Be sure to answer it. And don't tell anyone."

I went home and did what any good husband does—I told my wife, Jen. I asked her to come into the office for the call. She arrived the next day about five minutes before the appointed time. The guys had never met her. I was afraid if she came in the office and saw how productive I was, she'd expect that level of enthusiasm and efficiency at home.

Seeing Jen, everyone sensed something was up. The phone rang. I answered. It was the same colonel at the Pentagon, who once again verified my identity. Then the phone clicked, and I heard something about the White House secretary. The phone clicked again and someone said, "Staff Sergeant Giunta, this is President Obama." My heart was pounding so loud I was surprised the president didn't hear it. "Your packet came across my desk. I read it, and I want to personally thank you for your bravery. I'm going to award you the Medal of Honor on behalf of a grateful nation."

I was in a state of shock but managed to say, "Roger, Mr. President."

The president said goodbye, then the colonel came back on the line and told me to keep the news to myself until the White House announced it.

No way. During the call, word spread through the office, and by the time it ended, there were fifty people crammed around my desk. Somebody said, "Mr. President, for real?"

I tried to bluff and said, "Dude, I've been getting prank calls." Eyes rolled. They knew.

The White House ceremony was on November 16, 2010. I arranged for all the guys who were with me on the night of October

25, 2007, to be there, along with the families of those who had died. Josh's family came, as did Specialist Mendoza's. I met generals, senators, congressmen, and, of course, the president.

It was a solemn day, and I was receiving a great honor, but in some ways it felt like a bad dream. I've never been that comfortable being the center of attention.

I'm not a tall guy, not a strong guy, not a smart guy. I'm just a regular American guy who was inspired by his fellow soldiers. That's not modesty—it's the truth. If my actions that night showed anything, they show what many of us are capable of when bullets are flying and we're fighting for a country we love and believe in.

DORIS KEARNS GOODWIN

Author Doris Kearns Goodwin likes to tell the story of her first brush with the magic of Hollywood. After Steven Spielberg bought the rights to her book on Abraham Lincoln, Team of Rivals, *and Tony Kushner came on board as the screenwriter, they invited her to participate in the planning of the movie. To give him a feel for the reality of the time, Doris took Daniel Day-Lewis, who played Lincoln, to Springfield, Illinois, where they visited the house where Abraham and Mary had lived. Later, the producers took Doris to an abandoned pinball factory in Richmond, Virginia, the capital of the Confederacy, to see the movie set of the same house. Her reaction: "The accuracy of the details was meticulous: the rugs, the wallpaper, the lighting, the books on the shelf were the books that Lincoln had been reading. I felt as if I'd stepped back into 1865."*

The turning points in Doris's life that I recount for you are all about keeping an open mind and being willing to be proven wrong. We live in an era of polarization. We sort ourselves into groups and surround ourselves with the thinking of those who agree with us. Doris taught me how vital it is to open one's mind to the possibilities of the other side of any argument.

I owe much of the life I've had to baseball and Lyndon Baines Johnson. Let me tell you the story.

When I was six years old, my father taught me the mysterious art of baseball scorekeeping. I would listen to the Brooklyn Dodgers' afternoon game on the radio and record every foul, strikeout, and home run. When my father came home from work, he would take off his tie and jacket, he and my mother would have a Manhattan, and then the two of us would sit on the living-room couch and I would recount, in excruciating detail, every play of the game. Dad leaned in as I chattered away, making me feel like I was telling him a fabulous story.

And so, by age six, I was unconsciously coming to understand the magic of history—even if it's only an account of an afternoon's events—and the power of storytelling.

In our early sofa sessions I tended to blurt out excitedly "The Dodgers won!" or "The Dodgers lost!" This, of course, drained the drama right out of the ensuing narrative. I quickly learned that to keep Dad's interest and tell the best story, I needed a beginning, middle, and end. I learned that instinctively on the couch with my dad. He never told me that he could read all the details of any game in the next morning's paper. I thought that, without me, he wouldn't know what happened to our beloved Dodgers.

My love of history grew in high school. I visited Sagamore Hill, Theodore Roosevelt's home, and Franklin Delano Roosevelt's residence in Hyde Park. These were transcendent experiences for me. I saw FDR's glasses resting on a table next to his cigarette holder, as if he had just left the room and would soon return. I couldn't believe he was dead and kept saying, "He has to come back. He left his glasses." I wanted to bring FDR back to life. And I believe that, in essence, is a historian's calling: to bring people to life for later generations.

We lived in Rockville Centre, Long Island, a suburb of New York City. It was the 1950s, and the neighborhood emptied in the morning as all the men went off to work on the commuter train. The women were left behind to be mothers and homemakers. The houses were right next to each other, and our lawns were small, which created a quasi-urban environment for us kids, which we loved. The only thing separating my bedroom from my best friend's, who lived next door, was a narrow driveway. So we could chatter away at night when we were supposed to be asleep.

My father was an extraordinary man. His full name was Michael Francis Aloysius Kearns, and his looks matched his name—pure Irish—with a full head of sandy hair and twinkly green eyes. He was born in Brooklyn; his father worked for the New York City Fire Department. He had a younger brother and sister. When he was ten and his mother was pregnant with her fourth child, his brother was hit by a trolley car and died a few weeks later. His mother then died in childbirth, and his father committed suicide not long after.

So at age ten, my father was an orphan; he and his sister were split up and put in orphanages. He swore that he would go to work so they could be reunited and he could bring her up. And he did. He dropped out of school in the eighth grade and got a job. He had great mathematical ability and eventually got a job as a bank examiner for New York State. Over the years, he rose through the ranks to become superintendent of bank examiners. He died in 1972, when I was in my late twenties.

No one who met my father would ever guess that he'd endured such a traumatic childhood. He had a tremendously optimistic nature and was the most loveable man. He'd walk in the room, and it would light up in the reflection of those warm green eyes. I remember him telling me the most important thing you can have in life is an interest in other people. If you care about them, they'll care about you. His example in the face of tragedy is the most important lesson of my life.

My mother had rheumatic fever as a child, and it left her with heart damage. She had been ill from the time they got married, and they weren't able to travel because she was largely homebound. My father adored her, and they created a rich life within those restrictions, with close friends, card games, and trips to Brooklyn to see the Dodgers play. My mother died when I was fifteen.

My love of books and reading comes from my mother. Like my father, her education ended in the eighth grade, but she loved nothing more than getting lost in a book. She read to me a lot when I was little. I always asked her to tell me stories about herself when she was young, because I hoped that if I could keep her talking about the days before she got sick, she'd go back to being healthy. I didn't realize how unusual this was until my own three boys began pestering me to tell them stories about when I was young. Today my eleven-year-old granddaughter, Willa, is fascinated by stories of her father's youth. When she comes to our house, she heads to his childhood bedroom and wants me to tell her everything. I guess intense curiosity about your parents' childhoods qualifies as an official family trait. Again, it's about bringing history to life.

I left home to go to Colby College in Maine, and then I went on to graduate school at Harvard, where I studied government and history. I was interested in understanding the practical side of politics, and every summer I went to Washington as an intern. I worked at the State Department one summer and the House of Representatives another.

In 1967, I was selected as a White House Fellow. This program still exists today. It takes students right into the center of American governance and power. Colin Powell was a White House Fellow, as was General Wesley Clark.

This was during the Vietnam War, and I was active in the antiwar movement. In fact, a few months earlier, a friend of mine at Harvard and I had written an article attacking President Johnson and arguing for a third-party challenge against him in the 1968 presidential election. It was an idealistic article, arguing that a new party representing the poor and working class, minorities, and antiwar voters could sink LBJ's reelection bid. As luck would have it, the article—entitled "How to Remove Lyndon Johnson from Power"—was published in the *New Republic* just a few days before I began my fellowship. Not surprisingly, the article caused great consternation in the White House, and there were some who thought I should have my fellowship revoked.

But LBJ stepped in and said, "Just have her come down here for a year and if I can't win her over, no one can."

There was a dance at the White House to welcome the new Fellows. President Johnson came over and asked me to dance. As we were moving across the floor—towering Lyndon and diminutive me—he leaned down and whispered in my ear, telling me that I was going to be assigned directly to him. It was my first taste of Johnson's brilliant gift for intimacy, which he used to such spectacular effect in his dealings with Congress.

I was not, however, assigned to the White House. Instead I was sent to the office of the secretary of labor, a wonderful man named Willard Wirtz, who I became close to. We Fellows went to the White House several times that year, and whenever we were in the room with Johnson he never failed to smile and ask me if I had any questions. When LBJ was determined, watch out.

Then, on March 31, 1968, he announced that he wouldn't be seeking reelection. A couple of days later, Wirtz asked me to come to his office and said he had gotten a call from the White House: LBJ wanted me to work for him. When I got there, Johnson told me that, since he was removing himself from power, we could work together. So I spent the rest of my White House Fellowship in the White House.

Lyndon Baines Johnson was a force of nature, the most formidable, interesting, colorful character I've ever met. His storytelling was mesmerizing, profane, insightful, and earthy, his metaphors amazing. The full force of his personality didn't translate on television, especially when he was speaking from a teleprompter. To grasp the enormity of the man, you have to listen to tapes of his meetings with his cabinet and members of Congress. In public, he didn't trust himself not to start cursing, and so he stuck to the text. Which is a real pity, because the public, I believe, never understood the full measure of the man.

I developed enormous empathy for him. He opened up about his great sadness that his legacy had been truncated by the Vietnam

War. When he talked about passing the Civil Rights Act or the Voting Rights Act or Medicare, it was thrilling because he was happy. I was glad I wasn't working with him on the foreign policy chapters; I imagine that was a grim exercise.

Johnson's melancholy made me realize how easy it is for good intentions to go awry. Despite my early feelings about him, I developed a deep loyalty and affection for the man. After he died, I wrote a book about him, *Lyndon Johnson and the American Dream*. The book was published in 1976 and launched my career.

History is a great inspiration. It's telling stories about those who have lived before us, hoping that we can learn from their struggles and their triumphs. We find echoes of our own lives, lessons that resonate, solace and inspiration that help us get through hard times or push forward to a goal. And by speaking to our shared humanity and past, history unites us. I'm thankful that baseball and Lyndon Johnson opened that world up for me.

ALAN GREENSPAN

Alan Greenspan, who became chairman of the Federal Reserve, discovered early on that he had a knack for math. When he was five years old, he was able to add triple-digit numbers in his head within seconds. He likes to tell of how his mom often had young Alan perform this trick at get-togethers in front of friends, relatives, and neighbors. Alan had a favorite math teacher in middle school named Mr. Small. As a homework assignment, Mr. Small sent Alan into local banks to get deposit and withdrawal slips. This was Alan Greenspan's first association with banks, but obviously, not his last.

The defining moments Alan shared stuck in my mind because they are clearly about success and failure. So often we look at powerful, successful people and assume they got where they are today thanks to good luck, a helping hand, or some special talent. But Alan reminded me that often success comes after an initial failure. He reminds us that even when our dreams fail, happiness and fulfillment may be just around the corner.

My first job, well before I became the United States' chief banker, was as a member of a 1940s swing band that travelled the country and played the latest hits in smoky nightclubs. In hindsight, my progression from saxophonist to chairman of the Federal Reserve seemed highly improbable.

Born in 1926, I was raised in Washington Heights, Manhattan's northernmost neighborhood. The Heights earned its name because it is the highest natural elevation on the island, and for that reason George Washington set up his headquarters there during several important Revolutionary War battles. In my youth, the neighborhood was a bustling mix of middle- and working-class immigrant families, mostly Jewish and Irish.

My father, Herbert, worked on Wall Street as a broker. He was slender and taciturn. My mother, Rose Goldsmith, was small and pretty and kind. Both my parents were the children of Jewish immigrants from Eastern Europe.

My parents' marriage was not a happy one. Their temperaments were too different. When I was two, my parents divorced. After the divorce, my mother and I moved in with her parents, who lived nearby. My mother began to work as a saleslady. I didn't see a lot of my father.

The one great joy of my family was music. My grandfather was a cantor, and my mother sang and played the piano. She loved the standards of the day, songs by Jerome Kern and Cole Porter and Rodgers and Hart, as well as Yiddish tunes. One of the high notes, so to speak, was my uncle, Mario Silva, who changed his name from Murray Goldsmith in hopes people would think he was Italian. Small and rotund, Uncle Mario loved to sing opera and was a very accomplished pianist. He moved to Hollywood, where his hands appeared in many movies: when the star was supposed to be playing the piano, Mario's hands would be substituted in the close-ups. My uncle had a career doing what he loved, and his commitment to his craft made a lasting impression on me.

Music was in my blood, and I was eager to take up an instrument. I had a slightly older cousin, Claire, whom I liked a lot, and when she took up the clarinet, I copied her. I started practicing seriously when I was ten, which is a bit later than most professional musicians. Luckily I didn't know that.

I entered George Washington High School in 1940. The school was housed in a magnificent building that would look right at home on an Ivy League campus. The tower atop the school was being used by the US Navy as a lookout to spot any German submarines that might make their way up the Hudson or Harlem Rivers. One of my schoolmates was the son of recent German Jewish immigrants who had fled the Nazis; his name was Henry Kissinger.

I played clarinet in the school orchestra. My classmate Hilton Levy organized a dance band, and I joined. We played at school dances, proms, and other local functions. Our repertoire included "Bye Bye Blackbird," "Sweet Georgia Brown," and Glenn Miller's classic "In the Mood." I loved being on stage, watching people dance to the music we played. I also loved to dance myself, and wasn't half bad at the lindy hop.

I was becoming more serious about music, and began to consider it as a career. I signed up to study with one of the city's best teachers, Bill Sheiner. Sheiner's studio was in the Bronx, and he taught clarinet, saxophone, flute, and oboe. I took up the sax, which I loved. You can't teach talent, of course, but Sheiner was brilliant when it came to technique, and he demanded daily practice. He took my discipline to a new level. One of Sheiner's other students happened to be Stan Getz, who went on to become one of the all-time great jazz saxophonists. Stan's talent was obvious and abundant. In addition to having music in common, we came from similar backgrounds and became friends.

I graduated from George Washington High School in 1943 and entered Juilliard in the fall. It was there that I started to play piano; I later added the bass clarinet and flute to my roster of instruments. One day I got a call from the manager of the Henry Jerome Orchestra, a popular touring band at the time, telling me that Bill Sheiner had recommended me, and asking me to come in for an audition. I took the subway to midtown, auditioned, and was hired. I left Juilliard for the road. Even though I was only eighteen, I felt very mature.

I started touring with the band, which had about fifteen members, including Leonard Garment, who was about a year older than me and went on to become Richard Nixon's White House lawyer. We mostly travelled by train and played in hotel ballrooms and nightclubs. The longest engagement I remember was at the Hotel Roosevelt in New Orleans. Everyone would dress up, drink the latest cocktail, smoke endless cigarettes, and dance all night. The atmosphere was swank and sophisticated, and it was all very heady for a kid who grew up with three generations in a small apartment in Washington Heights.

The Henry Jerome Orchestra was good, but we were a second-tier band, below the giants like Artie Shaw, Benny Goodman, and Harry James. We wore matching suits with velvet jackets and black pants. We had one extended gig in Covington, Kentucky, at a hotel that, to my surprise, also housed an illegal casino. I think in some way we were a cover for the gambling operation. I learned a lot about human nature while I was in the band.

While we were touring, I helped my bandmates with their income taxes and other money issues. It became clear to me that I had a natural aptitude for money and finance.

What also became clear to me over the months of touring was that, while I was a good amateur musician, I was only an average professional one. I realized I had probably gone as high and as far as I could, and I wanted to be at the top of my field.

So I left the band. In retrospect I realize how much Stan Getz influenced my decision. All I had to do was listen to Stan to know I would never be that good.

I loved my years playing in the Henry Jerome Orchestra and think of it often. I still play the piano now and then, but that is the extent of my musical engagement. As I look back, I continue to be inspired by the strange and wonderful path that led me to where I am today.

LOU HOLTZ

When you see Lou Holtz for the first time, you might think he doesn't look much like a football coach. He is slender, wears glasses, and he talks with a slight lisp. But I've learned as many have that first impressions can fool you. Lou is a master motivator. He is the only coach in college history to have taken six different college football teams, all with losing records when he arrived at the school, to a bowl game by the second year and the only coach to take four different college teams to a top twenty ranking.

Since we first became friends in 1984, I have been guided by the defining moments and powerful influences in Lou's life that he has shared with me. Whether you love sports or have no interest, Lou's message totally transcends athletics: adversity is part of every life; the real question is what we are going to do about it.

I was born Louis Leo Holtz in Follansbee, West Virginia, in 1937. My parents lived in a cellar apartment—no refrigerator, no shower, just a sink in the bedroom to wash up in. We had so little that being poor would have been an upgrade. When I was very small we moved to East Liverpool, Ohio, a booming town in the pre-Rust Belt days, where my dad worked for the local bus company. He wasn't there for long, though. Soon after we moved, he shipped off for World War II, and the rest of my family—my mother, my uncle Lou, and my grandparents—was charged with taking care of me.

71

My father didn't return from war until I was in fifth grade, so Uncle Lou, who was a high school football player, taught me how to play sports. He even coached my first football team. On weekends, we would gather around the radio with my grandfather and listen to Notre Dame games. There's no question that my love of football came from my Uncle Lou. And from my father, who returned from the war and never talked about it, I learned my lesson in humility.

I spent much of my youth with my buddies, hanging out on Saturday nights at Dairyland Corner in town. My friends called me Sunshine, because I was a happy guy. I played football, but I didn't look much like a football player. I weighed about a hundred pounds and remember standing in line to be weighed as part of our physical and yelling out, "If I stand in this line all this time and don't weigh one hundred pounds, I'm going to be sick." I survived football in high school by learning as many positions as possible and filling in when anyone got hurt.

I was also expected to work part-time jobs to give some money back to my family. At an early age, I learned the importance of personal responsibility. It is what still fundamentally guides my thinking.

Back then, very few of us thought about going to college. My idea of life after high school was money in my pocket, a car, a girl, and a job at the mill. But my high school coach, Wade Watts, told my parents that I should attend college because someday I would make a good football coach. I had a good memory and had memorized the football playbook as thoroughly as my coach had. Even though I had no interest in college, my parents insisted. We argued back and forth. My mom and dad would say, "You are going," and I would reply, "I'm not." We continued this conversation for a time, eventually reaching a compromise. I consented to go.

I attended Kent State along with all of my high school friends— Bill Rouse, Bob Dorzy, and Bill Biern. We chose Kent State because it was close enough to hitchhike home. Despite my love of college football, I didn't join the team until my junior year. Now at 165 pounds, I was a small linebacker and had to work harder than anyone else on the team just to earn my spot.

After graduating in 1959, I attended Iowa University where I got a master's degree and was a graduate assistant on the football team. In 1961 I married my high school sweetheart, Beth Barcus. We moved to William & Mary, where I was an assistant coach for two years, and then to the University of Connecticut for two seasons.

My life with Beth and career in football was moving in the right direction. But things were about to change.

In February 1966, I was hired as a defensive backfield coach at the University of South Carolina. Unlike William & Mary and Connecticut, South Carolina didn't have faculty housing, so I bought a house, using every cent of our savings for the down payment. A month after we settled in, Beth and I woke up to a newspaper headline announcing that head coach Marvin Bass had resigned to take a job in the Canadian Football League. Spring practice for the team had already begun, so the school quickly hired Paul Dietzel from West Point to replace Bass. Dietzel brought his own staff with him. He interviewed me, but I sensed he was just being polite, and soon after, he told me he was letting me go. As I was walking out the door, Coach Dietzel stopped me and asked, "Lou, have you ever thought about going into a different profession?" He didn't mean that I couldn't coach; he just felt badly that I was unemployed and had a family to take care of. But it still hurt. At age twenty-eight, I was unemployed, had payments due on our house, no money in the bank, two young children, and a wife who was eight months pregnant.

Beth naturally rose to the occasion. Just weeks after giving birth to Kevin, she went to work as an X-ray technician. It was March, and no schools were hiring, so I spent three months as a stay-at-home dad with the two little children and an infant. My admiration for mothers skyrocketed.

To lift my spirits, Beth bought me a book to read, *The Magic of Thinking Big*, by David J. Schwartz. In the book, David wrote if you are bored with life and don't have a desire to get up in the morning and do something, you need to establish big goals for yourself. So I got paper and pencil and wrote down all the things I wanted to do. I wanted to go to the White House for dinner, be on *The Tonight Show*, see the pope, win the NCAA National Championship, and coach at Notre Dame. I wanted to jump out of an airplane, land on an aircraft carrier, race with the bulls in Spain, and hit a hole in one. The more I wrote, the more excited I got and before I knew it I had 107 things I wanted to do. Beth came home one day and I said, "Honey, look at this, 107 of these things and we are going to do every one of them." She said, "That's nice; how about adding one more?" I said, "Sure, what?" "Get a job," she answers. So we made it 108.

Not long after that, Paul Dietzel surprisingly offered me a job helping to run the scout squad. The offer came with a cut in salary—from $11,000 to $8,000—but I took it.

The scout squad stands in for opposing teams during practice and is made up of less-talented players. A good scout squad coach will research an opposing team and copy their plays in hopes of preparing the varsity team for the real game. My scout squad played a regulation game against South Carolina's freshman team, which was highly regarded, and we beat them. Coach Dietzel was impressed and I was promoted to defensive backfield coach. My salary was restored to $11,000.

Paul Dietzel was on the board of trustees of the coach's association, and he asked me to be the recording secretary. In January 1967, the association held its annual meeting in New York City. Coach Dietzel couldn't attend, so he sent me. One night there was a dinner, and Woody Hayes, Ohio State's legendary coach, was sitting at my table. He started to ask me all sorts of questions about coaching. I shared my ideas on specific plays, belief in teamwork and playing hard, and philosophy about setting standards of behavior and sticking to them.

The next day, January 6, was my birthday. It was a good one. I got two job offers—one from Georgia Tech and the other from Woody

Hayes. Georgia Tech's offer was better financially, but my family and friends pushed me to choose Ohio State. I visited the campus and spent two days with Coach Hayes. It turns out I'd been recommended to him before our dinner in New York, and our conversation that night had really been a job interview.

We won the national championship at Ohio State, and after a year, William & Mary offered me the head coach position. I was ready; I'd worked under some talented people and developed confidence in my abilities. I learned to look for intangibles when putting together a team. The number-one criterion I looked for is a love of the game. Football is about camaraderie and unity, not just height and weight and speed. Yes, talent is important, but it's the intangibles that create a cohesive team capable of supporting that talent.

I was head coach at William & Mary from 1969 to 1971. I then moved to North Carolina State for three years. After that I spent a year in the NFL as head coach of the New York Jets. It didn't take me long to realize I was better suited to college football.

In 1977, I moved to the University of Arkansas for six years and then I spent a year at the University of Minnesota. My agreement at Minnesota allowed me to accept one and only one job if it opened up: Notre Dame. Notre Dame was a dream job for me and I started coaching there in 1986. I coached at Notre Dame for eleven seasons and had a record of 100–32–2. We won the national championship in 1988 and went to nine straight bowl games.

In 1996, I retired and started broadcasting for CBS. I didn't think I would coach again. But two years later and forty-five years after being fired by Paul Dietzel, I returned to South Carolina, inheriting a football program that was 1–10 the year before.

It was a tumultuous first year at South Carolina. Beth had her second major surgery for throat cancer and they gave her a 10 percent chance to live. I am glad to say that she is fine now. My son, Skip, currently the football coach at Louisiana Tech, went into a coma because of a virus the week we played Georgia and we almost lost him. My mother died the Friday before we played Florida.

I was on an airplane for four days recruiting when we landed at Lady Island, Beaufort, South Carolina, to meet assistant coach Charlie Strong and talk to a recruit. There wasn't a refueling station at Lady Island and the pilot said, "Coach, while you visit Darnel Washington, we are going to fly eleven miles to Hilton Head to get gas and we will be right back. Leave your suitcase and hanging bag on the plane."

Charlie and I visited Darnel and returned to the airport. There was no sign of the plane. We found a guy who was preparing to take off in a single-engine plane and explained the situation. He said, "I got a report of a crash, and I'm heading out to search for it." It was our plane; during that eleven-mile flight, the plane crashed. One school pilot was killed instantly and the other was seriously injured and later died. We lost every game we played that year, going 0–11.

The newspapers started writing negative stories about the team. People were saying I was too old and finished as a coach. Life was so bad that one day a man approached me at the airport, asking, "Anyone ever tell you that you look like Lou Holtz?" I said, "Yes, it happens all the time." And he said, "It really makes you mad, doesn't it?"

Two of the most difficult periods in my life occurred at South Carolina. But the lessons I learned—first in 1966 and reinforced in 1999—have guided me all my life. In football and in life, adversity and misfortune are only temporary. After being fired by Paul Dietzel, I was rehired by South Carolina and four years later, I became the head football coach at William & Mary. And forty-three years later, after going 0–11, we rebounded and were ranked in the top twenty the following year, beating Ohio State in a January 1 bowl game.

I'm not special, and I'm not particularly smart. I haven't found any magical formula for success. But what I do know is, adversity is part of life, no matter who you are, what your age, and what you do. You will never outgrow or outlive it, but you can be motivated by it. As I have learned along the way, you have two choices in life: you either stay down or pick yourself up. In life and football, you can't count on anyone else picking you up. Georgia or Michigan State isn't going to call and say, "Coach, you don't have a quarterback, let me send you one."

MORTON KONDRACKE

Growing up, American journalist and author Morton Kondracke always wanted to be famous. So, it was a thrill for him, in later years, to appear in two motion pictures, both in 1996: Independence Day *starring Will Smith and* Getting Away with Murder *with Dan Aykroyd and Lily Tomlin.*

In reality, Morton's life was hardly a Hollywood tale. I include the turning points that Morton shared with me because they are about courage and strength. Morton reminds us that no matter how successful or powerful we are, there will be forces of nature we can't always control.

In 1967 I was working as a reporter for the *Chicago Sun-Times* when a friend introduced me to Millicent Martinez. A recent graduate of Roosevelt University, Milly was thin and beautiful, with olive skin and dark hair enlivened by a striking shock of premature gray.

When we met, Milly was working as a probation counselor in the juvenile court of Chicago. At that time judges often placed neglected or abused children into juvenile custody, where conditions were deplorable. Milly's job was to confront the judges and tell them they were sending good kids to what was basically a jail. Her efforts led to the practice being curtailed.

Milly's combination of heart, smarts, and energy dazzled and touched me. I fell in love with her—which surprised me. She wasn't what I had in mind for my future wife. I was young and ambitious and hoped to marry someone who could help me along the path to fame and glory. I was so shallow and determined to marry the likes of a senator's daughter or an heiress, I even engineered an end to the relationship. We had gone skiing. Milly was a terrible skier. After she had fallen for what seemed like—and might have been—the hundredth time, I started yelling, finishing my tirade with, "That's it, we're finished." We broke up.

Sometime later, I ran into Milly on the beach in Chicago. Once again, I was captivated by how dynamic she was. In spite of what I thought were my better instincts, I asked her to the movies. At the theater, a friend of Milly's happened to be sitting in the row in front of us. She turned around and exclaimed, "What are *you two* doing together?" Before the end of the evening, we were at that friend's apartment, drinking wine and smoking a little pot. We left at 2:00 a.m. It was raining, we were under an umbrella under a streetlamp, and I kissed her and I thought, "Okay, I get it, this was meant to be." I proposed. She said yes.

We had a small wedding at a chapel on the University of Chicago campus. We paid for it ourselves—it cost all of $400. For some long forgotten reason, we served watercress sandwiches.

Milly's mother, an American Jew, abandoned her as a child, and Milly was raised by a Mexican foster family in Chicago. Surprisingly, Milly's mom attended the wedding, as did, of course, all of her foster family. Her foster mother, Annie Villarreal, gave her away. Her father, Refugio Martinez, was a Mexican and a communist labor organizer for the meatpackers' union. When Milly was a child, he had a stroke that left him disabled. During the McCarthy era, deportation proceedings were begun against him. He fought to stay in this country, and his case went all the way to the Supreme Court. He lost, was deported to Mexico, and died the next day of another stroke. I think her father's experience helped forge Milly's passion for the underdog.

In 1968, the *Sun-Times* transferred me to Washington, where I became a White House correspondent. Milly got a job at the juvenile court in Arlington County, Virginia. Once again, she fought for the children in her charge. But work wasn't enough. She always had an extracurricular cause.

In 1985, Milly found a cause close to home. Much closer. I liked my wine. I liked it with dinner, I liked it with lunch, and I liked it in between. At some point my drinking crossed a line—I was driving drunk, my work was suffering, and I endured nasty hangovers. Milly staged a one-woman intervention, forcing me to acknowledge that I was an alcoholic. I quit drinking.

The following Christmas we were in Vermont, where we went for the holiday every year. Our daughter, Andrea, was applying to colleges, and one day Milly was sitting at a table writing checks for the application fees. "Something is wrong with my handwriting," she said. I looked at the checks and her handwriting looked fine to me, but she was insistent that she had less control in her hands.

A couple months later, she developed a tremor in the little finger of her right hand. It worsened, and her doctor wasn't able to give us a definitive diagnosis, so we began to see specialists. One gave her a prescription for Symmetrel, a drug developed to treat influenza that was showing promise as a treatment for Parkinson's disease. When she discovered this, Milly threw the pills away. She refused to accept the possibility that she had Parkinson's.

This was in 1987; Milly was forty-one years old. That's young to be stricken with Parkinson's.

We went to see every specialist that would see us. The Mayo Clinic initially told us it wasn't Parkinson's after all, but essential tremor, which is a benign syndrome. But the symptoms kept getting worse. We went back to Mayo, and they finally diagnosed Parkinson's and started Milly on Symmetrel.

In part because of her father's strokes, Milly was terrified of any debilitating illness. One evening she told me, "I'm going to become disabled and pathetic, and you're going to leave me."

I took her in my arms and said, "I'm not going to leave you no matter what. I'm here for you. You can depend on me."

Up to that point in my life I'd been obsessed with career and status, determined to climb the greasy pole of Washington journalism. After Milly's diagnosis, I told myself, "If you do nothing else right in your life, do this right."

And so began a seventeen-year ordeal. We went doctor shopping; we went drug shopping. Even though Parkinson's afflicted 1.5 million people in those days, the disease was relatively unknown. Milly was determined to fight both her own disease and society's indifference.

For all the increased visibility and research, Parkinson's remained (and remains) an incurable disease, and Milly's decline continued. In a cruel twist, she didn't have classic Parkinson's but a horrible variation called multiple system atrophy, in which bodily functions and organs shut down. She began to fall, often with no warning. We were living in a two-story house in Chevy Chase, and one day she fell backward down the stairs. We moved into a one-story condo.

We went to Cornell Hospital in New York City to see a doctor who was doing experimental brain scans. They showed the progression of the disease—Milly's brain literally shrank. Swallowing became increasingly difficult, and a feeding tube seemed inevitable. Then she lost the ability to walk and talk. We communicated on a computer or an alphabet board.

Milly's journey continued. We heard about a brain operation called pallidotomy, which involved using a heat probe to locate and destroy small sections of the brain that are found to be abnormally active. Milly said, "I want it, I want it, I want it!" She had the surgery, and if it helped at all, the improvement was slight and temporary. She also underwent deep brain stimulation (DBS), which is now standard treatment for symptoms of Parkinson's. Sadly, DBS only made her symptoms worse.

Then her body chemistry went haywire. She was hospitalized for a dangerous sodium imbalance. They normalized the imbalance, but the treatment had devastating side effects that left her completely disabled. She was practically in a vegetative state. I brought her home, and hospice began to care for her.

In the summer of 2004, I decided that it was time to let Milly go. I called our daughters, Andrea and Alexandra. I told them I was going to remove the feeding tube and asked them to come home.

The night after I made this decision, fate intervened. I was asleep. Milly was in her room down the hall, being watched over by a hospice caregiver named Graelanda. I was woken by Graelanda's cry of "She's dead!" I got up and went to Milly. Her body was still warm. Her quiet death was a great blessing.

It was a difficult seventeen years, but throughout it all, Milly made me a better person and she inspired me. She inspired everyone whose life she touched. Our dear friend Terry Shaffer, many years earlier, put it best: "Everybody becomes a better person because of Milly."

I had those words chiseled on her headstone.

TED KOPPEL

Ted Koppel likes to tell the story of how he lost his first job. Fresh out of college and newly married, Ted got a job as copyboy for an AM radio station in New York. His salary was $90 a week. When his new wife, Grace Ann, got pregnant, Ted went in to see R. Peter Strauss, owner of the station, to ask for a raise. Turned down, Ted quit. Years later, he thanked Peter Strauss for his parsimony, because "if he hadn't been so cheap I may never have gone to work for ABC and had a career as a journalist."

I was impressed by the influences in Ted's life because he so clearly understands and communicates it in relationship to the world around him. Often, we are caught up in the minutia of our daily lives and we see ourselves inside our own little bubble of experience. Ted reminds us that occasionally we need to step back and see ourselves as actors in a bigger play, upon a larger stage.

I'm a product of the twentieth century—it defines the arc of my family and my career.

My mother, Alice, and father, Erwin, were late Victorians; my father was born in 1895 and my mother in 1899. They were both born in Germany and were Jewish, but they were German first, with a capital G.

My father served four years in the kaiser's army. He went on to become a successful businessman, founding what became the third-largest tire company in Germany. In his mind, he was the ultimate German citizen. Then one day in 1936, his name appeared in a Nazi newspaper on a list of Jews who had been stripped of their German citizenship. He was devastated.

My father understood that his world was about to be shattered, but he refused to leave Germany while his mother was still alive. After she died in 1937, he left for England. My mother joined him the following year. They were married there and then moved north to Lancashire, where the British government had asked him to manage a rubber factory. He had expressed concern about his status should war break out. The home secretary wrote him a letter assuring him that he was a guest of the Crown and that nothing untoward would happen to him or his family.

World War II broke out in the fall of 1939. In February 1940, I was born in Lancashire. Two months later, my father was arrested by the British and sent to an internment camp on the Isle of Man. I suppose his detainment made sense: German spies might present themselves as German Jews to infiltrate British society. In any event, the British were taking no chances, and they arrested most of the Germans in England.

My mother, who didn't speak English, was left alone with a two-month-old. Eighteen months after his arrest, my father was released and the three of us moved to London.

There is a powerful lesson in my parents' story. At the start of the twentieth century, they felt secure about their position in society, about the stability of that society. Then events threw all of that into a cocked hat. In fact, I doubt my mother and father would have married if it hadn't been for World War II. My father was an overachiever, young and wealthy, something of a professional bachelor, and he travelled a lot for business and pleasure. He was simply working too hard and having too much fun to want to settle down. But the war forced his hand.

For her part, my mother was a talented musician—she played piano, had a lovely voice, and sang with some of Germany's most renowned conductors. Her father died when she was very young, and she and her brother took over the family coffee-wholesaling business. She was accomplished in both business and the arts. Of course, both endeavors came to an abrupt end.

My father was forty-five when he was arrested by the British. He was at the peak of his professional life and had achieved great success. Suddenly, all of that was gone, and he was stateless—his German citizenship had been revoked and he was ineligible to apply for English citizenship (he did become a British citizen after the war). Moreover, he wasn't allowed to work, so his talents lay fallow. This was a terrible fate for a man with his energies.

After my father's release, we lived on the proceeds from the sale of the few pieces of jewelry that my mother had managed to smuggle out of Germany. We didn't have much money, but I never felt deprived. In the days of rationing, we were fortunate in that the German palate was accustomed to cuts of meat that the British shunned. Our milk was delivered with half an inch of cream at the top, and my mother would save that for two or three days and then whip it into butter. She would also buy all the butcher's chicken necks for a few pence and make a wonderful and warming chicken soup.

After the Allies won the war in 1945, my father began making frequent trips back to Germany to try and reclaim his factory and houses. He was gone for months at a time, and, in 1950, my parents decided that they really had to be together in Germany. So I was packed off to Abbotsholme, an English boarding school. This marked a major turning point in my life.

The school was still suffering from postwar deprivation. There were no indoor toilets, so we used outdoor stalls that were essentially sandpits. There was very limited hot water. We took one (very quick) cold bath a week. The food was iffy at best; the big treat of the week was the rabbit stew. Other popular menu items were baked beans on toast and Welsh rarebit—basically grilled cheese, easy on the cheese.

Abbotsholme aped the traditions of better known English public schools. The upperclassmen were called prefects and would be assigned an underclassman my age; his designated "fag." The word had no sexual connotation. A fag would clean the prefect's room and fix his afternoon toast. Being one of only two Jews at the school and the son of Germans only five years after the end of the war did nothing to enhance my status. Boarding school was not a happy place for me, but I did learn independence. It would become a trait that would serve me well in life.

Being an outsider in an English boarding school not only taught me independence but it taught me to be aware of vibrations in the air, danger signals, subtle clues. These experiences were invaluable later in life as a journalist.

I can trace my ambition to be a journalist to my earliest childhood. My parents lived and suffered the consequences of war, and the time we would gather around the radio listening for news made a lasting impression on me.

There's a quote from Dante that both John F. Kennedy and Martin Luther King Jr. used to paraphrase: "The hottest places in hell are reserved for those who, in times of great moral crisis, maintain their neutrality." That's always struck me as being a rather elegant, if tough, definition of what it takes to be a good journalist. That is, the ability not to align yourself on one side of an issue or another, but to view events with a certain degree of impartiality. Because of my childhood, that was a hard lesson to learn but always my source of inspiration.

One of the most moving moments in my career came ironically on an episode of *Nightline* that I didn't think was going to be particularly memorable. I was interviewing a young woman who was the product of an affair between a Vietnamese prostitute and an African American soldier. The offspring of these relationships were known as "children of the dust." In this case, the father, after raising a family of his own in the United States, felt honor-bound to go back to Vietnam and find his daughter. He brought her back to the United States, and she came on *Nightline*. I asked her what it was about the United States that surprised her the most. She answered, "The sky." I said, "The sky? I don't understand. It's the same sky as in Vietnam, isn't it?" She answered, "Oh no, back home I was much too ashamed to look up." It was an emotional gut punch and a lesson that stays with me to this, and every, day. I, too, am an immigrant to the United States and, since moving here, have never had to feel ashamed to look up.

MIKE KRZYZEWSKI

He is one of the greatest college basketball coaches of all time. But what sport did he and his school buddies love on the playgrounds of Chicago? Pro wrestling. Mike loves to tell how he and his buddies would dress up and pretend to be famous pro wrestlers. His favorite was Édouard Carpentier, a Canadian wrestler who won several championships and was known for his flying maneuver, the rope-aided twisting headscissors.

What I learned from Mike hit home. As I was growing up, my grandmother would respond to every story I shared with her by saying, "Well, Bernie, pretty is as pretty does." As Mike now shares with us, sometimes our greatest influence in life comes from simple homemade advice, which some of us can too quickly dismiss or take for granted.

I grew up in inner-city Chicago, in what was basically a little Ukrainian and Polish village surrounded by a big city. Many of the local shops sold Polish products. There was a Polish newspaper, and you often heard Polish spoken on the streets. It was a safe, tidy community that looked out for its own; life was centered around work, the Catholic church, and family.

My parents were the children of Polish immigrants. My father, William Krzyzewski, had a tenth grade education and was an elevator operator at the Willoughby Tower office building downtown.

My mother, Emily, worked as a cleaning woman at the Chicago Athletic Club at night while I slept. My mom had only an eighth grade education. In fact, she went to eighth grade twice. I remember asking her, "Ma, what happened?" and she said, "Oh, Michael, the teacher loved me."

I had one brother, Bill, who was three and a half years older. For elementary and middle school, Bill and I went to St. Helen's parochial school; we also went to St. Helen's church, so we were there six days a week. We could have taken classes in Polish, but my parents didn't want us to study it. They wanted us to assimilate and were afraid we would end up with Polish accents that might hurt our future job prospects.

Mom had an infectious sense of humor, and at family get-togethers she was our Lucille Ball, a real jokester. She just loved to make people laugh. She was also a meticulous housekeeper; our flat was organized and spotless. We didn't have a lot of money, but she was brilliant at making ends meet and even tying them in a bow. She had two dresses. Her wardrobe philosophy was simple: I don't go out that much; two dresses are enough. She loved to bake, and when she made chocolate chip cookies, she carefully rationed the chips: three to a cookie. Years later, when I started coaching and making a good living, she added a fourth chip.

My dad worked long hours. I didn't see a lot of him when I was growing up—he would come home exhausted, eat, and go to bed. Dad grew up in Pittsburgh, and when he moved to Chicago as a young man, he started to use the last name Kross. There was a lot of ethnic discrimination at that time, and he didn't want to hinder his ability to support a family. He served in World War II under the name Kross. When he died, at the age of fifty-nine of a cerebral hemorrhage, the government, because he was a veteran, provided a tombstone. It read "William Kross." Mom left it that way to save money. When she passed away in 1996, my brother and I got them matching headstones that read "Krzyzewski."

Dad always carried a lot of change, and it would jingle in his pocket. When he was getting ready for bed, he had a habit of hanging his pants on his bedroom doorknob. One day when I was eight, I wanted some money to buy an ice cream bar. Dad was asleep, so I snuck into his pants pocket and, as quietly as possible, took a fistful of change. I went and got my ice cream, sure Dad wouldn't miss the change. It turned out he had a lucky coin in that pocket, one that he never spent. Well, I had spent it. He asked me about the missing coin, and I denied everything. Dad looked disappointed. After retreating to my room and giving it some thought, I confessed. Dad put a hand on my shoulder and told me, "If you need something, you should ask for it. But never steal and never lie." I haven't stolen or lied since.

We kids had a lot of freedom in those days. In the summer we'd head out in the morning and be gone all day, except for a possible midday appearance to grab some lunch. A group of us would meet at the playground of a local public school, Christopher Columbus School; we called ourselves the Columbos. We played sports and games until we were exhausted. No parent or coach was organizing our games, picking teams, or making decisions. I learned basic leadership skills on that playground. We Columbos worked things out among ourselves because we had to. We also explored the city, taking the bus to Wrigley Field or downtown.

St. Helen's school was within walking distance of our house. For high school I was going to follow in my brother's footsteps and go to Archbishop Weber High, which was in northwest Chicago, two bus rides away from home. The night before school started, Mom said, "Michael, please sit down. I have something to talk to you about."

"What do you want, Ma?"

"Just sit down and listen. Tomorrow starts a new part of your life."

I was a feisty Chicago kid, I knew it all, and I answered, "Yeah, I know. I'm going to high school."

"I want to make sure you get on the right bus," Mom said.

"Look, Ma, I know. Damen to Armitage, Armitage to Laramie, Division to Grand, Grand to Laramie."

"That's not what I'm talking about, Michael. In high school, you're going to meet new people and learn new things. Before you get on someone's bus, make sure the driver is a good person. If you're the driver, only allow good people on your bus. Stay away from people who are going to get into an accident, or drive in the wrong direction. To be successful in life you need to be on a bus filled with good people."

Her words were so simple, but so profound. It's the best advice I've ever gotten, and it's guided my actions and decision making ever since.

I played basketball at Weber and did pretty well, making the all-state team. In my senior year, several colleges recruited me, including Creighton University, a Catholic school in Iowa, and the University of Wisconsin. Then coach Bob Knight at West Point contacted me and offered me a scholarship. I had no desire to be in the army and turned him down. My parents couldn't believe my decision.

The kitchen was the sit-and-talk room in our house. When Mom and Dad didn't want Bill or me to understand what they were saying, they'd speak Polish. Well, for two weeks I heard a lot of Polish coming from the kitchen. It was blah-blah-blah, stupid, blah-blah-blah, Mike! You could call it ethnic pressure. I finally got the message and accepted West Point's offer. The Polish ceased. Getting on that West Point bus was probably the single most important decision of my life.

Mom lived to see me win a couple of national championships at Duke. Ten years after she died, in 2006, my wife and I established the Emily Krzyzewski Center in Durham in her honor. Our mission is to help academically gifted kids from low-income families get the extra help they need to do well in school and get admitted to college. We call it the K to College Model.

Mom's advice to "get on the right bus" was a turning point in my life and has inspired and guided me every day of my adult life. I consider it my responsibility to share her simple but profound words with people wherever I go. My mom cared deeply about people—I know that she would take great comfort in knowing that while she never got a high school education, her wisdom and knowledge still resonates with the kids today.

STEW LEONARD JR.

Stew Leonard Jr. will be the first to tell you: going into the family business is both a joy and a trial. He joined his father's company fresh out of business school. One of the first things Stew Jr. did was convince his father to set up a series of strategy meetings so he could share what he learned in college. Stew's father couldn't make one of the first meetings, so Stew called him to ask for his thoughts.

"Dad, since you can't make the meeting, is there anything you want me to tell the group?"

"Yeah, tell them to make sure every ear of corn we sell is fresh picked that morning!"

"Dad, this is a strategy meeting. We're discussing important strategic issues facing our company. Do you have any big strategic issues you'd like me to mention to the group?"

"Yeah, tell them to make sure every ear of corn is fresh picked that morning."

The defining moment in Stew's life that I share serves to remind us that tragedy can either defeat us or allow us to reevaluate and repurpose our lives.

I learned the business at my father's knee, and when I got out of business school I was eager to prove to him, to the world, and to myself that I could not only meet the high standards he had set but build on what my dad had done. I think it's safe to say I was work-obsessed from the very first day.

Dad had built the business from scratch. He opened the first Stew Leonard's in Norwalk, Connecticut, in 1969. There was a farm for sale in a great location, but the owner would only sell to someone who promised to keep farming some of the land and to take care of her animals. Dad agreed and had the brilliant idea to use the animals to start a petting zoo. He began with seven employees, and he just kept making the shopping experience more enjoyable, adding singing and dancing animatronic animals, employees in farmer costumes, and a general sense of fun. Today we have nine stores with over two thousand employees. We're in the *Guinness Book of World Records* for having "the greatest sales per unit area of any single food store in the United States." And Tom Peters, in his best seller *Passion for Excellence*, recognized Stew Leonard's as one of the best companies to work for.

I dedicated myself to the company and for seven years, life was good. But life can change in an instant, and on New Year's Day, 1989, that's exactly what happened.

My extended family was at our home on St. Maarten. We were celebrating our daughter Blake's third birthday. I was out by the pool, up on a ladder, inflating and tacking up the balloons that our twenty-one-month-old son, Stewie, was handing up to me. My wife, Kim, was inside, baking the birthday cake. I can still smell that cake and hear the kids' laughter as they played around the pool. It was a great day.

Then I looked down and Stewie wasn't there. I assumed he had gone into the kitchen to lick the last of the cake batter from the bowl, something he loved to do. I went inside. No sign of Stewie. Kim and I checked his bedroom; his teddy bear was alone on the bed. We started to panic and ran outside. That's when I spotted a flash of yellow, his T-shirt, floating in the pool. I scooped him up; he was unconscious. I started CPR immediately, but there was no response. Kim and I ran to the car and raced at eighty miles an hour to the nearest hospital, about fifteen miles away.

The doctor came out and told us: it was too late. Kim and I just sat there holding hands, staring straight ahead, in shock. Even at that moment, I knew everything would be divided into "before" and "after."

Kim and I went through a long grieving process. It took time, and, in addition to grief, there was blame, anger, and resentment. It caused some friction in our marriage; for a little while we each blamed the other for the tragedy. And you can't help but feel like a victim: Why did this terrible thing happen to me? Sometimes well-meaning people would say, "You'll get over this." But one of the lessons I learned is that you don't ever get over a trauma that deep. You can't simply wrap it up, leave it behind, and move on with your life as if it hadn't happened.

Stewie's death was an accident; my obsession with work didn't contribute to his drowning. After years of doubt, I came to understand and accept this as best I could. But it doesn't lessen the guilt I still feel today. After business school, nothing was more important than work. My priorities were work related. I put work before my family and I justified it by saying, "It is what is best for the family."

I remember not long after I started working I got a very heartfelt offer from my maternal grandfather, who had immigrated to this country from Germany. Family meant everything to him. He called me one day and invited me to come to Germany with him. He wanted to show me the town where he had grown up, where my roots were. I told him, "Gee, Grandpa, I'm just so busy, I can't take off a week and a half to travel." He was hurt, but he disguised it. I didn't take the trip. He died not too long after that.

Today my life has changed. More to the point, I am a different person. I look back on my grandfather's offer all the time, and I say to myself, "Boy, do I wish I had taken the time." It meant so much to him, and nobody would have missed me a bit.

I hug my four daughters and my wife a lot longer and tighter now and spend more time with extended family. Those are obvious lessons. And I could tell you that I care more about people now. That would be obvious, too. Our company was always people friendly, so that always came with my job description. What has changed in me is a lot deeper and a little harder to explain than the obvious lessons. My life is slower now. Oh, work is fast, that's not what I mean. What I am trying to say is that I look at people differently now. When I look at someone today, I am overwhelmed with the thought, "What's happening in their life?"

What Stewie's death taught me I guess falls somewhere between empathy and perspective. I'm proud of my work ethic, but the fact is, I was born with advantages and privilege. Most people aren't. When tragedy hits, it's very humbling. You realize your basic humanity, and that it's something we all share.

I was talking to one of my daughters recently about college. She was obsessing on getting into a top-flight school. I reminded her that she was lucky to be going to college. It's not necessarily a given. We have a lot of young employees who work the cash registers at night to earn enough money to go to a community college part-time.

My cousin Danny told me a great story about perspective. He runs our store outside Hartford. He's worked there for thirty years now, and he works hard. He has a little beach house up on Cape Cod, and not too long ago he bought a used twenty-eight-foot boat. It's a nice boat. One day he was out on the harbor with his wife, and nearby was this sleek sixty-foot yacht. His wife said, "Honey, wouldn't you like to have one of those?" Danny pointed at the fishermen on the banks and said, "They're probably looking at us and saying the same thing right now."

As I said, it is a little hard to explain. It is an ongoing process for me, and years later I am still trying to figure it all out. What I can say clearly is that I am inspired to be a better person now, and the reason is this: I want to do it for Stewie.

MARY MATALIN

Much to the amazement of most everyone in Washington, Mary Matalin and James Carville have been happily married for almost twenty-three years. Like most couples, that doesn't mean they don't do battle at times. The topic they fight about most is animals—Mary loves them, and James is indifferent at best. Mary and James also had fights about the Iraq War. When Mary went to work for Vice President Dick Cheney during George W. Bush's first term, she told me (maybe tongue in cheek) that James didn't speak to her for months.

The influences Mary shared with me offer a lesson to those of us who want to do great things in this world: the greater the odds against success, the greater the reward.

I was a miracle baby . . . or so goes the family legend. My mother, Eileen, had suffered five miscarriages and was told she couldn't have children. Then I came along. Maybe my safe arrival shouldn't have been such a surprise. It was the early 1950s, a time when everything seemed possible.

As all mothers are (and I know of what I speak!), mine was a little bit overprotective of me. As for my father, Steve, he was the first son of a first son, and I was the first grandchild and—oops, a girl. No problem for "the miracle baby," because contrary to their pre-feminist era, my parents had the same expectations for me that they would have had for a boy. They believed that there was nothing I couldn't do if I put my mind to it. This wasn't feminism to them, it was Americanism.

My mother was of Irish and English descent, arriving early to the new country; my father's family came from Croatia at the dawn of the twentieth century. My grandparents came from different cities in then-Yugoslavia, but met on the boat over. They were ever after together and built a life in America unfathomable had they stayed in the "Old Country." My paternal grandfather never learned English very well; my grandmother finished eighth grade yet ended up as chief dietitian at a hospital at a time when most women didn't work. The American Dream of upward mobility is in my genes. I was raised on a steady and heartfelt exposition of American exceptionalism.

After my maternal grandmother died at the unbelievably tragic age of forty-two, my folks moved into their own home. Soon, I was joined by a baby sister, Irene, and brother, Steven. My dad worked at the iconic United States Steel (USS). He had an intense work ethic and that American drive for constant self-improvement and life-long learning. While working full-time and raising three babies, he attended Illinois Institute of Technology and received a degree in mechanical engineering. My mother was an equally hard worker. I remember sitting on the floor with my baby siblings watching her iron, cook, and clean nonstop, and all manner of holding down the home front while dealing with three little ones.

We lived in a tight-knit ethnic community. Our neighborhood was literally a melting pot. Poles, Italians, Germans, Serbs, Lithuanians, Croatians, Irish, and a bevy of other European immigrants. Our common values were common sense, aspiration, and community. We believed it the obligation of every person to take care of him or herself first. The thinking was: you can't take care of your family if you can't take care of yourself. Family, of course, was the core unit in that place and time. There was a common reluctance to seek outside help in the face of problems. If a challenge became overwhelming, we went to the church or the larger community. The government was the recourse of absolute last resort, and I can't recall one single person on any government subsidies.

I was a tomboy. Being a girl seemed boring. It's not that I didn't like clothes and all that, but I liked what the boys did—the competition of sports, general rowdiness, riding bikes with no hands. Boys had more freedom, were funny, boisterous, and less self-conscious. I remember thinking to myself as a teenager: my goal in life is not to be bored.

Once all the kids were in school, my mother decided she wanted to augment the family income. Women in that place at that time didn't have "careers." Her father had told her she couldn't go to college or even nursing school. His message: get married. She did, but that didn't curb her curiosity and ambition. A voracious reader, she gave herself a darn good well-rounded education. And she wanted to work, no matter what her father said. She went to beauty school at night and then opened a salon in our basement. My mother was a decent hair stylist, but she was a *natural* at teaching and managing. She got a job teaching at her beauty school. Then she became head teacher. Then she bought her own beauty school. I started working there when I was eleven—greeting customers, scheduling appointments, taking money, and balancing the books.

Though I didn't realize it at the time, my political views began to form when I was a young teen. Every time my mother wanted to expand her business, some regulation stood in her way. The government intrusion at the steel mill where my father and all my uncles worked was legendary and counterproductive. No matter how well intentioned these regulations were in their everyday execution, I could see how they dampened growth and job creation.

Slowly I began questioning my hippy-liberal sentimentality, which was all the rage then. In our blue-collar Democratic 'hood, Republicans were considered country club elitists.

It was at Western Illinois that I got actively involved in politics. I majored in political science, but it was my experiences that had the greatest impact on my thinking.

I had to work to help pay my tuition and earn spending money. I was always shocked to receive paychecks significantly depleted by local, state, and federal taxes, too often causing a steady diet of PB&J!

By the 1992 presidential campaign, I had become deputy campaign manager for President George H. W. Bush. We were running against Bill Clinton, whose chief campaign strategist was James Carville, whom I had been dating for a year. Needless to say, our across-the-aisle romance set tongues wagging. What people didn't understand was that we're both passionate, even fiery, people and—although our politics are different—we each felt we had found a kindred spirit.

Clinton won the election, of course, but I won James, or he me, and I didn't make it easy! We were married in October 1993. Rolling eyes were added to the wagging tongues. Twenty-three years later, we're still together. He's never boring.

Our backgrounds could hardly be more different. James is from deep south, rural Louisiana. I'm from Chicago. I grew up with traffic jams and steel mills, amidst a sea of ethnic names. He grew up in a town named after his family! When he was a kid, James didn't ride a bike—he rode a horse. When we started dating he didn't own a car.

Neither one of us is good at compromising—and I don't mean politically. But that's why separate rooms were invented. We give each other lots of space. In addition, we were older when we got married—I was forty and James was forty-nine. We knew who we were, and we each had our own career.

That said, we have profound philosophical differences. James believes I run to the sound of a gun, but I like to help people to handle their own problems. When he sees something that needs fixing, he wants to raise money. He wants to find a community-based solution. James is a redistributionist who thinks Jesus said, "Give the poor your clothes." I think Jesus said, via St. Paul, "If you don't work, you don't eat."

However, we both believe it's more important to give your time, your sweat, and your heart to a challenge than to write a check.

So, what binds us is stronger than what divides us. Neither of us believes in moral relativism. There are values that should not bend to the whims of time and trends. There is time-honored and honed rationale for justice, for mercy, for honesty. These days, people seem to lie with impunity, as if stating something—often and loudly—makes it true. That's bullshit. Truth is truth. James and I have the same sensibilities about right and wrong, fairness and loyalty. We're iconoclasts; if and when we are out of sync with much of the world, we each remain inspired by our upbringing and still in sync with each other.

CHRIS MATTHEWS

Like so many young people with an interest in politics and political affairs, Chris Matthews headed to Washington, DC, looking for a job. He wanted to write speeches, so he went to Capitol Hill and started knocking on doors. After several weeks, he got a job working for Senator Frank Moss of Utah, a liberal Democrat. To get that position, as Chris tells it, he had to agree to a patronage assignment with the US Capitol Police. The deal was he would work in the office during the day answering legislative mail, then put on his uniform and .38 Special for the 3:00 p.m. police shift.

I was both surprised and impressed by the turning points in Chris's life. As his influences and defining moments show, we can often change the direction of our lives when we expand the boundaries of our comfort zone.

I grew up on the quiet outskirts of Philadelphia. Our little town of Somerton, which bordered on Bucks County, was surprisingly rural. We had farmhouses all around us, cows grazing in the field behind. My four brothers and I lived in a safe, unexciting world with all the privileges of private school, piano lessons, and a summerhouse on the Jersey shore.

It was also, now that I look back, a fairly insular world. All our friends were Catholic and middle class. Our parents' lives revolved around the weekday rituals of Holy Name Society, sodality, and Knights of Columbus. I never once shared a classroom—not in grade school, high school, or even when I went up to Holy Cross—with an African American or someone of another religion.

It was only after college that I began my progress into a larger world. With the help of a generous assistantship, I began work on a PhD in economics at the University of North Carolina. The perfect college town, it lived up to its name as "the southern part of heaven." It was a good life in Chapel Hill. By the end of my first year, I'd achieved enough academic success to win a National Defense Education Act Fellowship. Had the world outside not intervened, that award would have taken me on to my doctorate and from there to life, in all likelihood, as a college professor.

By the spring of 1968, however, I was forced to make a decision—a big one. Facing 1A status in the draft, I considered the options. One of my housemates was about to get a direct commission as a US Army finance officer. There was also the prospect of becoming an army public information officer. I thought it would help me get started in journalism, a career alternative I suppose was brewing in my head at the time.

Fortunately, a first-rate option arose. A young recruiter for the Peace Corps came to the UNC campus carrying with him a brochure about a new program in Swaziland. It dealt with small business development in the about-to-be independent country in southern Africa. Finally, I would have a way to put my interest in economic development into action.

That September, I left for Baker, Louisiana, a small backwater town north of Baton Rouge. It's where the Peace Corps had chosen for our training site and, it being just four years after passage of the Civil Rights Act, was redolent of Jim Crow. A laundromat not far from our campus had a glazed message on its window: "Whites Only." One of my fellow volunteers, a tough individual from Bayonne, New Jersey, got pistol-whipped by a white deputy sheriff after refusing to leave the blacks-only bar he owned. Such rigid segregation—enforced down there in both directions—would have struck me as improbable had I not witnessed it up close.

Other local hangouts were more welcoming to us. A short walk from campus stood a saloon named the Mustang. As a salute to his new customers the owner changed it—I assume temporarily—to LiHashi, the siSwati word for horse. We were by then on a strict "no English" diet, well into high-immersion language training.

In late November, the first batch of us headed off to Africa.

I was soon escorted to my assignment in the southern province of the country by the minister of commerce, industry, and mines. A shrewd politician who had spent part of his life working in the South African gold mines, he wanted to show off his new "trade development advisor" personally.

My housemate, Cliff Sears, an architect from Chicago, and I were assigned to a house in Nhlangano, an old Afrikaner town that looked like Dodge City in a western movie with its boardwalks running up and down the main street. In our apartment at the edge of town—a former nurses' quarters—we enjoyed some Third World luxuries: running water, even if it was cold, and a modern toilet. Most Peace Corps volunteers get neither. My additional perk was a shortwave radio, which I bought locally. On some evenings the BBC and the Voice of America were my only company out there.

Fortunately, Cliff and I, like most of the others in the group, became inveterate readers. This is one of the unrecognized advantages of not having a TV set in an entire country.

My area of responsibility was, as I said, the southern province of Swaziland. It covered a quarter of the country. My assignment was to help the two hundred small traders in the province improve their business skills. To get around, I had the use of a Suzuki 120 motorbike. When I entered a new area, I could tell from the surprised if friendly greetings that I was the first white person most of the local people had ever seen up close.

I developed a ritual for my visits to a trading store. I would look at the shelves to see what products were for sale. Except for the larger stores, the usual stock in trade included sugar, tea, and big bags of ground corn called "mealy meal." I would introduce myself to the owner and say in siSwati—which is very similar to Zulu—"I'm working for the government. I am here to help you with your business." Invariably, I would be greeted with the offer of a "cold drink"—a Coke or Fanta—even if there was no refrigerator for miles.

We would then get down to business, often a process of showing the owner how to better keep his books or how to set his prices so as to maximize revenue.

Life on the African roads was not always so orderly. There are snakes in Swaziland. I learned to stomp as I walked home on moonless nights. I didn't want to get bit by a snake, especially a black mamba. A bite from this aggressive reptile is fatal.

I had heard many stories about the black mamba, about it jumping into the backs of moving station wagons, or chasing horses. It can move, any book on the subject will tell you, at incredible speeds.

One day, driving through a stretch of desert we called the Valley of the Doomed, I found all this confirmed to me at frighteningly close range. The heat was so intense late that afternoon that vapors rose from the dirt road ahead as if it were laid with tarmac.

Suddenly, what looked like a black line appeared ahead and to my right. It stretched half the width of the road. Recognizing the dreaded black mamba, I swerved to the left just as the snake reared up at full length right at my window.

As I jammed on the brakes, I was sure it had made it through the window, that it was inside the car and on the attack. Gary Rowse, a pal of mine from Los Angeles, was sitting in the backseat and saw it all. Fortunately for both of us—including the Swazi business association leader in the front passenger seat—Gary quickly and happily reported that our black mamba had been thrown backward by the force of our passing car. He was back there on the road somewhere heading back into the bush.

There were, of course, joys to where we were in the world. Surrounded by South Africa on three sides, we were limited in our travels outside the country. There was, however, one great opening for adventure. It lay an hour hitchhike to the east in Mozambique. Its capital, then called Lourenço Marques, had all the atmosphere of Ernest Hemingway's Spain—romantic and lively, with outdoor cafes, Portuguese bullfights, modern movie theaters, and perfect beaches. There were 200,000 European expatriates living there, and it hummed with cosmopolitan flair and a hint of intrigue. The sight of soldiers lingering at the outdoor cafes served as evidence that the country was in the midst of revolution.

During my second year in Swaziland, I took my month-long vacation hitchhiking alone up through East Africa. I made it all the way to the foot of Mount Kilimanjaro in Tanzania, a distance of 1,600 miles. I passed landscapes right out of *Tarzan*, especially a wide escarpment on the road to Lusaka, the capital of Zambia. I arrived at Victoria Falls by night as I walked across the bridge just below it. I fished in a giant lake nearby with a white Zambian and his African wife. I saw Africa in a way most people never do. And in my two years over there I never worried about my safety, which is something most people have trouble believing.

In December 1970 it was time to come home. For me, this meant travelling up through East Africa a second time. In Mombasa, Kenya, which I loved, a local movie theater was playing *Butch Cassidy and the Sundance Kid*. Seeing Paul Newman and Robert Redford on screen in Africa was a perfect transition to coming home to America. I could sense in that film how our country's popular culture had changed in just two years. The opposition to the Vietnam War had grown. The bad guys were now the good guys.

From Kenya, I headed to Israel where I spent a month on what became something of a spiritual journey. Living in an Arab hotel above the Old City of Jerusalem, I lived in three worlds: the Arab world inside Damascus Gate, the first-run movie theaters of West Jerusalem, and the holy places of my Christian religion.

Finally, after other stops in Cairo, Cyprus, and London, I arrived home in the United States.

Isn't it interesting how life can teach us where to go? Had I not gone into the Peace Corps in 1968 and spent two years in Africa, I believe my life would have been far different. Those two years changed my outlook. There I was, for the first time in my life, out there on my own, thousands of miles from the familiar, working with people I would have otherwise never known.

Somehow it opened my own world. I gained a future filled with possibility and promise. I saw firsthand the power of simple kindness. I gained faith in the family of man. Under the African sky, I was inspired and I found a future.

GEORGE MITCHELL

Politicians in Washington aren't always known for putting the public good before their own personal interests. Which makes the following story even more amazing to me. In November 1993, Senator George Mitchell introduced a healthcare reform bill in the United States Senate. In March of the next year, Mitchell decided not to seek re-election. A month later, Justice Harry Blackmun retired from the Supreme Court. President Clinton called Mitchell and told the senator he wanted to submit his name to replace the retiring Justice Blackmun, probably a once in a lifetime opportunity. Mitchell thanked the president, but said he was still deep in the healthcare negotiations and if he accepted the position, the negotiations would fall apart. The president understood and appointed Stephen Breyer.

The defining moments and influences in George's life are very much a part of today's public and political discourse. Who are we, and what are our values? In the story that George shared with me, I found a truth: we will be ultimately judged in this life not by who we are or what country we come from, but by the values we decide to live by.

My story is uniquely American. My paternal grandparents were born in Ireland and came to this country in the late nineteenth century. They settled in Boston, which is where my father was born. Sadly, his mother died shortly after his birth, and his father couldn't take care of him and his siblings, so they were placed into Catholic orphanages in the Boston area.

There was a practice back then in which nuns would take groups of orphans to rural Catholic churches. At the end of mass, the children would stand in front of the congregation and parishioners were invited to come forward, take one or more of the orphans by the hand, and walk out with them. The trips were called weekend specials, and there were no formalities, no papers, no legal process. The system was ripe for abuse, and farm families would often take children and put them to work, not sending them to school. The practice was later regulated, but not before my father was taken from Boston to Bangor, Maine, where he was claimed by a childless Lebanese American couple, who moved to Waterville shortly thereafter.

Then a town of about 20,000 people, Waterville had a thriving textile industry. My father's adoptive parents opened a small general store in a working-class neighborhood next to one of the mills. The family lived above the store. My father went to school for a few years, but he left in the fourth grade to go to work.

My mother, Mary née Saad, was born in a village in Lebanon and raised Catholic. Two of her older sisters preceded her in immigrating to the United States. One of them, who immigrated with her Lebanese husband, ended up in Waterville, living next door to my father and his parents. The couple had a young daughter they had left behind until they could get established. When they were ready, they asked my mother, who was eighteen and still living in Lebanon, to bring the girl over.

In 1920, my mother arrived in the United States with her niece. She soon found work in a textile mill and spent the next forty years working in mills, becoming a highly skilled weaver. Her story is a good illustration of the economic prosperity at the time—here was an uneducated, inexperienced young woman who didn't speak English, and yet she found a job soon after she arrived in this country.

Living next door to each other, my parents met, fell in love, and married. They had five children—four boys and then a girl. I came along in 1933, the youngest of the boys.

I'll never understand how my mother did it, but she raised five kids while working the graveyard shift from 11:00 p.m. until 7:00 a.m. I can still see her coming home covered with lint—back in those days, the working conditions in the mills were deplorable, and every surface was covered in a layer of lint. In addition, the floors were oil-slicked and slippery, so the workers shuffled around. And the noise was deafening; you literally couldn't hear someone who was six inches away. My mother worked under those conditions for all those years. Yet every morning she was there to see us off to school, and every afternoon she was there to welcome us home. She also did the shopping, cooking, washing, and cleaning. We all learned self-reliance from her example.

My mother was uneducated in any formal sense and couldn't read or write English. In fact, she could barely speak it—she had a heavy accent and often used the wrong word. But she had a great sense of humor about her limitations. When she mispronounced a word and was corrected, she would exaggerate her mispronunciation for laughs. She was religious—we never missed Sunday mass—and she lived the gospel every day with her selflessness, her cheerfulness, and her generosity. She was simply the kindest, best, strongest person I've ever known. And the greatest influence in my life.

We lived in a neighborhood called Head of the Falls, named so because it was perched above a sharp drop in the Kennebec River, with a waterfall and a dam. Directly across the river was a large paper mill. Back then, no one wanted to live next to a river. The Kennebec was heavily polluted, smelled terrible, and was covered with scum and foam. When I was six years old, my father proudly moved us to a house that was only a few hundred yards away, but those yards were away from the river and across the railroad tracks. We moved, literally, to the right side of the tracks. There were seven of us in that house, which only had one tiny bathroom.

My siblings and I all worked from an early age. I started at five, delivering papers, shoveling snow, mowing lawns, washing cars, and working as a janitor at the Boys' Club. My parents never made a lot of money, but we were always well fed and made do with hand-me-down clothes; I never felt any stigma because half the town was in the same situation.

My father, who was smart but uneducated, worked for the local utility company. When I was a senior in high school, the utility company eliminated his division and he lost his job. Being unemployed was humiliating for him, and he fell into a depression. He finally got a job as a janitor at Colby College in Waterville. Within a few years, he was head of the school's maintenance crew.

My three brothers were talented athletes and had gone to college on athletic scholarships. I wasn't as good at sports as my brothers; in fact, I wasn't as good at sports as anybody's brother. Since my father was unemployed during my senior year of high school, there was a question about whether I would be able to go to college. I was about to apply for a job at the local paper mill when he told me that his former supervisor at the utility company, Harvey Fogg, wanted to talk to me.

I went to see Mr. Fogg, who knew about our family's situation. He asked me what I was planning to do about college. I told him I was unsure. He said, "You've done well in high school. Have you thought about going to my alma mater, Bowdoin?"

I was surprised, grateful, and intimidated. Bowdoin had a terrific reputation, but it seemed beyond my means in every way. "I haven't considered it," I admitted.

"I think you should," he told me. "In fact, I've made an appointment for you with the director of admissions."

A week later, I set off for the Bowdoin campus. Since my parents didn't own a car and there was no money for the bus, I hitchhiked, setting off early in the morning armed with two sandwiches my mother had made for me. I walked the two miles from our house to the highway and quickly got a ride. When I told the driver my story, he took me right to the campus. So I got to Bowdoin five hours before my appointment. I later joked that I never got lost on campus because I'd spent a whole day memorizing every building and landmark.

I finally met with Bill Shaw, the director of admissions.

After a few minutes of friendly chat, he asked, "Would you like to come to Bowdoin?" I said I would and then explained my financial situation.

He asked, "Are you willing to work?"

"Yes."

"If you're willing to work, we'll find some work for you. Take this application, go next door, fill it out, and we'll get back to you."

And so I was admitted to Bowdoin. My first week there, I went to see Mal Morrell, the athletic director, about a job. The Morrell family owned (and still do) a large heating oil and building materials company in central Maine. Mal sent me to their offices, and I was hired. I'll never forget my first day on the job. The foreman asked me if I could drive. I had my license but had only been behind the wheel twice (and one of those was my driving test), but I answered, "Yes."

The foreman said, "Take that flatbed truck up to Thomaston. Go to the cement factory and load up ninety-pound bags of dry cement."

Thomaston was fifty miles north, up heavily trafficked Route 1. And it was a huge truck. I was panicked, but I didn't want to lose the job before I'd started. I gulped, climbed up into the cab, and tried to figure out the gearshift. The foreman asked, "Is anything wrong?"

"Oh no, I'm fine," I managed. Well, I drove that truck at about five miles per hour on the way up and about two miles per hour on the way back.

I spent my first two years of college working at Brunswick Coal and Oil. Then Mal Morrell arranged for me to get the basketball program concession. Basketball was very popular at Bowdoin and in the local community. The games were well attended and everyone got a program with the season schedule, news about the players, and advertisements for local businesses. I basically produced the program in lieu of a scholarship. I went out and sold all of the advertising, arranged the printing and distribution, and kept the difference. It was a good education in the basics of business and profitable enough to pay most of my tuition.

I also served as the steward of my fraternity, Sigma Nu, which entitled me to free meals. And I was a proctor in the dorm, which got me a free room. So I cobbled together a very inexpensive college education. But it never would have happened without the mentorship of Harvey Fogg, Bill Shaw, and Mal Morrell. They reached out and took a chance on me, the son of uneducated immigrants from Ireland and Lebanon.

I could have never guessed, growing up as I did, that my life would lead me to be the majority leader of the United States Senate, recipient of the Presidential Medal of Freedom, and chairman of the Walt Disney Company. The bedrock of my life, the foundation I've returned to again and again, has been the work ethic and undaunted spirit of my family. Their uniquely American legacy has guided my actions and provided inspiration every day of my life.

LIZ MURRAY

Liz Murray lives a perfectly normal life. She is married, has two beautiful children, Liam and Maya, and is busy pursuing a master's degree in psychology at Columbia University. But when you read of her harrowing childhood, you realize quickly what an achievement "normal" can be.

In my conversations with Liz, I found one of the greatest lessons of all: don't let life get the best of you.

I was about six years old, playing on the living room floor of our apartment in the Bronx. My mother was in the kitchen cooking, but she wasn't making brownies or spaghetti. She was cooking up the heroin she was addicted to.

I heard my mom coming down the hall, and then she appeared in the doorway, a horrified expression on her face. She held out her arms, which were covered with track marks and bruises, and said, "Don't ever do this. I don't know how to stop, but don't you ever start. You'll break my heart if you do." Then she started crying.

That scene is emblematic of my childhood. I was born in the Bronx in 1980 to drug-addicted parents.

They did drugs every day. There was rarely enough food on the table, the house was a mess, and they had little time for my older sister, Lisa, or me. If they weren't high, they were chasing their next fix.

My parents shot up in the kitchen with the door closed. One of my earliest memories is of pushing my stroller in front of the door, climbing into it, and waiting for them to come out. When they did, their eyes were electric and they had blood spattered on their arms. At that age, I didn't know what they were doing—but I knew it wasn't good.

Then they began leaving the kitchen door open. Lisa and I would go in, and there were Mom and Dad sticking needles into their arms. It got to the point where we just ignored it; if we wanted something in the kitchen we'd go in, grab it, and leave.

My parents were sick and caught in their addictions, but they were also incredibly loving. Some nights, Mom would sit at the foot of my bed and tell me about her dreams for me. She'd say she loved me and cover my face with kisses and say, "You and Lisa are the best things that ever happened to me." My father—who had been in a PhD program before the drugs took hold—would take me on long walks and talk to me about science and literature and history.

But their disease always won in the end. Dad had family on Long Island, and although they never visited, they sent us cards on our birthdays and on holidays, often with a $5 bill inside. On my tenth birthday, Mom took my birthday money and left the apartment. I figured out pretty quickly what was going on, and I waited for her to come back.

She soon reappeared with her heroin, which came in little tinfoil packets. She headed into the kitchen and I followed, yelling at her, calling her a terrible mother and a terrible person. I had never done that before. She looked at me in a kind of panic and then scooped up the heroin, a syringe, the rubber tubing she used to tie off her arm, and she ran into the bathroom. I thought she was trying to get away from me and get high in peace.

I followed her. She threw the drugs in the toilet, flushed them down, and started crying. I started crying too, and pretty soon we were on the bathroom floor hugging each other as she pleaded, "I'm not a monster, I just can't stop. I love you, I love you." As she held me in her arms, I could feel how much she loved me and how much she hated herself.

After that I began noticing things. If I hadn't had a hot meal in twenty-four hours, my parents hadn't had one in two or three days. I may have needed a new winter coat, but Dad's sneakers were held together with duct tape. I began to understand that people can't give you what they don't have. Or as I've heard it said, "If you need a dollar and I have a dime, I just can't help out." My parents were scrounging for pennies. Knowing this helped me, even at that age, not take my parents' disease personally. I loved them, and I knew they loved me.

Luckily there was a responsible adult close by. His name was Arthur. He lived in the apartment above us, and he was a friend of Mom and Dad's. He was a sixties kind of guy, who rode an old Triumph motorcycle, wore leather jackets, and had two dogs and an adorable girlfriend. Arthur also loved to go fishing. My parents sometimes had screaming fights that Arthur could hear up in his apartment. In the middle of the smashed bottles and the hurled curses, we'd hear a knock on the door and there would be Arthur, fishing poles in hand, asking me if I wanted to go on an adventure. We'd drive up to a lake in Westchester or across the Hudson River in Rockland County.

As we sat with our lines in the water, Arthur would ask me how I was feeling, but in a casual way that made it easy to talk. He always told me my parents were sick, but that they loved me, and that their disease wasn't their fault. He had tremendous compassion for them.

I missed a lot of school all through my childhood. Social service agencies got involved a couple of times, and I was put in foster care for a brief period. I learned how to game the system by lying to social workers and truancy officers. My main concern was protecting my parents. I would go to school regularly for a couple of months and then let it trail off again.

When I was about twelve, my parents were tested for HIV, and both were positive. Their health slowly declined. Mom went into the hospital when I was fourteen, and it was pretty clear she wasn't going to come out. We lost our apartment, and Dad moved into a shelter. Lisa moved in with Mom's father, who was abusive, but I refused. So I was homeless.

I thought at first that I was just couch surfing, bouncing from one friend's house to another. I had a close friend named Chris, who was a runaway, and every night we'd knock on a different door. Then one night no one would take us in. Their parents had had enough. So we rode the D train all night, huddled next to each other, grabbing sleep when we could. We had our backpacks with our socks, toothbrushes, and journals, which were very important to us. I also carried my favorite picture of my mother, taken when she was seventeen. She's standing on a street corner in Greenwich Village, homeless herself, a runaway, with a big smile, alive with freedom and promise.

I learned the survival tricks of the homeless. Aside from the subways, I slept in Central Park and in dark corners of tenement hall-ways. Most tenement buildings have a landing just inside the door to the roof, and these were prize spots because you were unlikely to be discovered. Before bunking down for the night, Chris and I would steal a blanket off a clothesline. In the morning, we would wake up early and look for a restroom where we could brush our teeth and hair, wash our faces, and try not to look too much like bums.

I heard about a place called the Door that served homeless kids. It was located downtown, on the western edge of Soho, and offered health care, meals, pantry packs filled with food, therapy, and a place to hang out. Chris and I would pick up packs filled with Cheerios and peanut butter. We also begged for spare change and stole from supermarkets.

It took a while for it to sink in: oh, I'm homeless. It was adventur-ous and fun at first. There was a sense of freedom—I'd escaped a bad situation. We were very punk rock. Chris had a pink Mohawk and wore a dog collar, and my hair was purple. The only color clothing we wore was black. Then it stopped being fun and got depressing.

We would go to friends' houses, see the looks on their faces, know we were an inconvenience, mooches. We couldn't plan past our immediate needs: a few bucks, some food, a place to sleep.

My mother was fading away in the hospital. I would go and visit her and then head off to find someplace to spend the night. Seeing her that sick made me sad, but also triggered something profound. Curled up on a hard floor or nodding off on the subway, a voice inside my head started to nag me. I called it the "what if" voice. It would say things like, "What if I got an apartment?" or "What if I went back to school and got my life together?"

I think all of us have some variation of the "what if" voice. It's easy to tune it out in the light of day, when we're busy with all the prosaic challenges of life. But no matter how much I was struggling, I could hear its echo.

Because seeing her was so painful, I started to put off visiting Mom in the hospital. She was ravaged by AIDS, skeletal, covered with sores, and filled with regret, guilt, and sadness. I'm not proud of it, but a month went by without me visiting her. Then one day she died.

She was buried the day after Christmas. I'd just turned fifteen. I begged for change on the street so that Lisa and I could pay for a cab to the cemetery. There was no funeral. She was just one of many rectangular pine boxes going into the ground. Her name was written on the box in black marker—it was misspelled. They'd also written the words "head" and "feet" on either end of the box.

After my mother's body was lowered into the ground, Lisa and I went back to a friend's house in the Bronx. We were in a familiar place, but I was seeing it with different eyes. A group of us were sitting around, all rebellious and angry. One friend was complaining that his mom had burned the pork chops the night before. Another was going to quit her job because her boss was a jerk. Someone else was dropping out of school. As I was listening, all I could think about was how grateful I was. My mom was in a pine box in the cold earth. I was young and had choices. What else did I really need?

I thought about all the poverty on the planet, all the starvation. I had this American concept of poverty, but what I went through and saw around me would probably look like a good life to tens of millions of people around the world. Nobody was handing them pantry packs. I knew I was going to be okay.

The first step was getting back into school. I asked other kids where they'd gone to high school. Then I would call 411 from a pay phone and get the number of the school. I'd make an appointment with the admissions office, and write the time and address down in a small notepad. I went from one interview to another. I got turned down everywhere because of my truancy record and my age. I needed to start as a freshman, and I was the age of most juniors. A lot of the admissions people advised me to get a GED, telling me that I was hopelessly behind.

The interviews tapped into my deepest insecurity. I'd always felt as if a wall separated the rest of society from people like me. I had an us-versus-them attitude. It wasn't exactly a chip on my shoulder, more a sense of living in different worlds, different realities. I always felt like I was looking in the Christmas windows at the fancy department stores—you can look but you can't touch.

One afternoon I found myself standing outside Hunter College on the Upper East Side. They had just turned me down for their Urban Academy. I was frustrated and disheartened. I had one appointment left, at Humanities Prep School in Chelsea. I had a choice: I could either take the subway down to Chelsea or head up to the Bronx, get a slice of pizza, and hang out with my friends. I didn't have enough money to do both, because getting down to Chelsea and then back up to the Bronx meant two subway fares. And I was hungry. I stood there thinking: "Pizza or interview? Pizza or interview?" Then my "what if?" voice piped in: "What if this is the school that will take you?"

I got on the subway and headed to Chelsea. Humanities Prep was housed in the basement of an enormous building that dated to the early twentieth century; the rest of the school was called Humanities High. I walked into the building and followed the signs to

Humanities Prep. I was nervous; I'd been doing so poorly on these interviews. Plus, I was scheduled for a group interview and was late. When I walked into the office, the other kids were sitting at tables writing essays. So I sat down and wrote an essay.

Then my name was called, and I walked into a smaller office. Sitting behind a desk was this white guy in his fifties, wearing glasses and a tweed jacket and looking like he taught Shakespeare and lived in a library. I was there in my full punker armor. I crossed my arms and talked to the floor. He told me his name was Perry. He was friendly, but said I was late and that he didn't have time for me. I apologized and told him I'd written the essay. That seemed to catch his attention, and we talked a little bit, but I was having trouble making eye contact. Then Perry pointed at a skull-and-crossbones pin on my backpack and said, "That's a nice pin. Where can I get one for my jacket?"

"Oh, so you think you're funny?"

"I know I'm funny," he replied, not missing a beat. Then he started to tell me these really terrible corny jokes. Despite myself, I started laughing. As we kept talking, something happened between us, some chemistry, and I just opened up and my story poured out. Without realizing it, I'd uncrossed my arms and was looking him in the eye. Perry sat there listening, concerned and curious.

I believe listening is an act of love. The only other grown-up who'd ever listened to me like that was Arthur. You know when someone cares. Perry cared.

The one thing I didn't tell him was that I was homeless. I was afraid if I told him the truth he would have to refer me to child welfare. I gave him a friend's address and told him I lived with my dad and his girlfriend.

I even told Perry about my "what if?" voice. I said, "What if I come to school here, get straight As, and go on to college?"

"Do you realize how much work that would take?"

I was taken aback. I was used to people pitying me. Most people who go into social work are sincere and caring, but they can be overly sympathetic. They treat you like you're broken, a victim. Perry immediately challenged me.

"I'll make you a deal," he said to me. "I'm going to admit you, but I'm going to mentor you and hold you accountable."

I'd never had anybody mentor me or hold me accountable. Perry lived on the other side of the wall, and he was reaching out to me. Then we stood up, and I found out that Perry was a hugger—not my style. But he hugged me, and it felt good.

I enrolled at Humanities Prep as a freshman. My first semester I signed up for five classes. Perry reminded me of my age and all the catching up I had to do, and I added two more classes. I was doing a whole school year each semester, which would allow me to graduate in two years. I aimed for straight As, but sometimes I came up short. I'd tell Perry that I got a B+, and he'd say, "That's fine for anyone else. But you came here to get all As." Then I'd go back to the teacher who'd given me the grade, do some extra work, and get it revised up to an A.

I was lucky because the teachers cared about education. Perry, who founded the school, had recruited them. He'd been an English teacher at Humanities High, which was overcrowded and had a high dropout rate. The teachers called a meeting to discuss possible solutions. One of them said, "Why don't we start an alternative high school in the basement, and we'll give the failing students a half day and the teachers can leave early. We can call it Failure High." There was a lot of laughter in the room. Perry didn't think it was funny.

He stood up and said, "I dare you to make an alternative high school that actually meets these kids' needs." Someone challenged him to do it, and he said, "I think I will." So he put a memo in all the teachers' mailboxes asking for help. He got one response. It was a start. Instead of going to alternative high schools and studying their models, Perry went to both private and public schools that had high graduation rates and were teaching kids Shakespeare and calculus. He drew up a model for Humanities Prep and then went out and recruited teachers who cared.

The result was a faculty that taught hard but fair. The reason I was able to do my homework even though I was homeless was because the teachers stayed at school until the janitor locked them out at night. They weren't paid for those extra hours. There was a huge room called Prep Central, where you could work on assignments. The teachers' desks were there, so you could ask for help at any time. This was nirvana for a homeless kid, especially because there were also couches in the room. I could stay late, study, get help, use the computers, and sneak in a nap.

Humanities Prep became my safe harbor. I didn't tell anyone that when I left at night I was heading to a hallway around the corner or to the D train. I carried an alarm clock and when it rang I'd find a bathroom, clean up, and head to school hoping no one could tell.

In the fall of my second year at Humanities, Perry took his top ten students on a field trip to Boston. We had a great weekend, and we finished the day with a visit to Harvard. I was walking through Harvard Yard with my backpack on. Inside it was the photo of my mom, my journal, my socks, and my toothbrush. Perry took a picture of us in front of the statue of John Harvard. As we were leaving, I looked at the students walking across the yard, wearing expensive clothes and Harvard sweatshirts, talking and laughing, and the wall went back up.

Perry realized what was happening. He leaned over and said, "You know, Liz, it's a reach but it's not impossible. Why don't you apply?"

As so often happened when Perry spoke to me, something shifted inside. Suddenly the wall seemed less daunting, and I said, "I will."

"I'm going to hold you to it."

Then I found out how much tuition was. I didn't have money for a turkey sandwich. So I began to apply for scholarships, including the New York Times College Scholarship Program. Most of the applications asked for an autobiographical essay that discussed any obstacles you've overcome. My reaction: "No problem!" I applied to Harvard, Brown, and several other top schools.

Near the end of my second year at Humanities Prep, Lisa and I got an apartment. I'd had a summer job at NYPIRG—New York Public Interest Research Group. They're the people with clipboards who stop you on the street and ask you to sign a petition to protect the environment and make a donation while you're at it. Most of my fellow clipboarders were college kids on break, and I was this oddball homeless person, but I ended up doing really well. We earned 38 percent of what we collected. I worked hard and saved my money, determined to get off the streets.

I couldn't work my last semester at Humanities because I had eleven classes, so I made a deal with my sister, who worked at the Gap. I paid all the move-in fees, and she was responsible for the rent. We moved in, and she lost her job a week later. The phone was going to be turned off. The eviction notices started coming. We were living on pantry packs from the Door. At the same time, I was doing my college interviews. I was starting to miss a lot of classes because we were trying to get on welfare so we wouldn't get evicted, and those office visits involved a lot of waiting.

In an effort to cut down on missed classes, I managed to schedule an appointment at the welfare office, my Harvard interview, and an interview at the New York Times College Scholarship Program on the same day. I tried to make myself presentable—I wore slacks I'd bought at the Salvation Army and I borrowed my sister's peacoat even though it was missing a few buttons. The welfare office was the first stop. They turned me down.

I went from there to my Harvard interview, which was held at a fancy midtown law firm and was conducted by a woman who was a Harvard alum. I felt it went pretty well. Then I walked across town to the *Times* building. I didn't know how prestigious the *New York Times* was—I'd never read it. I took the elevator up to the interview room. The other applicants were sweating and hyperventilating. The first thing I noticed was a tray of donuts that everyone was too nervous to eat. Not me—when I saw free food my survival instinct kicked in. The receptionist told me to help myself, so I grabbed three or four donuts.

I was called into the interview, which was conducted by about eight people. The mood in the room was very serious—I felt like I was appearing before a jury. There was a box of tissues on the table, so I guessed a lot of applicants cried. I starting taking the tissues and wrapping up my donuts while I told them my life story. Pretty soon we were all laughing, except for one woman who was crying. I told her, "I'm not crying, and it happened to me." After the interview, they sent me to the cafeteria for a free lunch. I left thinking *New York Times* people were solid.

I went back to school and quickly forgot about the interview. We were begging the landlord not to evict us. I got a phone call two days before our phone service was going to be cut off. It was the *Times* telling me I'd won a scholarship. I screamed my head off. They asked me to come in for a picture. After the group shots, they pulled me aside and asked me for a solo picture.

The next day the *Times* published an article on the scholarship winners, with my picture and my story. When I walked into school the next morning, there were all these strangers waiting for me, offering help with the rent, handing me tins of cookies they'd baked, clothes they hoped would fit—some just hugged me. It happened the next day and every day that week. Many of them said to me, "You touched my life." Two women came to our apartment loaded down with IKEA furniture, which they assembled. Other people stocked the refrigerator. These were people from the other side of the wall. Then I was accepted at Harvard. The wall was crumbling.

We're all busy and caught up in our personal struggles and projects, but when we take the time to listen, to care, and to reach out, humanity blooms. Arthur and Perry and my teachers and my friends and total strangers taught me the world is filled with good people who do good things every day. They have inspired me to be one of those people. I hope my mom is proud of me.

SCOTT O'GRADY

The world into which Scott O'Grady was forced to parachute was one wracked by violence. It was the former Yugoslavia at the height of the Bosnian War. Bosnians, Croatians, and Serbians were locked in a chaotic battle of atrocities. There were death squads and concentration camps. Mass executions took place. People were burned alive in their houses. There were systematic rapes. Estimates of civilian killings carried out by death squads were at least 250,000. But O'Grady lived to tell his tale of six days in Bosnia.

Of course, when you talk with Scott, you can't help but be amazed by his ordeal behind enemy lines. It is clearly a powerful defining moment. But there is another layer to Scott's story, one often forgotten. It is this: consider carefully the decisions you make, aware that at any time you may find your choices being tested.

I was born in Brooklyn, New York, in 1965. My father was a US Navy surgeon—Dr. William O'Grady. When I was five he was assigned to the navy hospital in Long Beach, California. We drove there cross-country. We lived off the base, and one thing I remember clearly is seeing the Marine sentries salute our car when we came to the station. I was very proud of my father. He was later deployed to a hospital ship in the Gulf of Tonkin during the Vietnam War. He operated on wounded soldiers brought in by helicopter.

My dad had also gotten a pilot's license, and the first time I was ever on a plane was when he flew me from Long Beach Airport over to Catalina Island in a little Cessna. I thought flying was fascinating and a great adventure. As I got older I began dreaming of being a military pilot. It was pretty much all I could think of by the time I was twelve. I did a lot of reading—about the different service branches, about how you needed to go to college before you could train as a pilot. I settled on the US Air Force. I liked all the types of aircraft the air force had, but another reason was that I really didn't care for the idea of landing a plane on a runway that moved. And the idea of being on an aircraft carrier at sea for six or nine months at a time didn't appeal to me either. So I chose the air force. I studied hard. I applied to all of the military academies, and wouldn't you know it—the one I got into was West Point. Well, the army doesn't fly fixed-wing aircraft, just helicopters. I didn't want to fly a helicopter.

So I went a different route and attended college at the Embry-Riddle Aeronautical University in Prescott, Arizona, where I enrolled in the Reserve Officer Training Corps—ROTC. I did well in my studies and excelled in ROTC, which ended up providing a scholarship for my final two years of school. I was commissioned as a second lieutenant in the US Air Force when I graduated, and headed off to train as a jet pilot. It was truly a dream come true.

After I finished my training to fly the F-16, which also included survival school, I got my first assignment: Korea.

Next I was sent to Germany, and there I began to fly combat missions. We got deployed out of Germany to Turkey and I flew ten combat missions over northern Iraq. Our orders were to protect the Kurds living in that region. Then we were redeployed to Aviano, Italy, where we began flying missions over Bosnia. There was a civil war going on there. We were part of a NATO operation that was enforcing a no-fly zone established by a United Nations resolution. This put us in a complicated position, since we were not actually one of the warring factions. All of the integrated defense systems of the former

Yugoslavia were still in place: airports from which attacks could be launched, communications posts, and control operations centers. They had surface-to-air missile sites and the large-gun emplacements we call antiaircraft artillery that could be used to shoot at us. And our rules of engagement were this: If we were shot at from a ground source we could not shoot back. We could not attack in order to defend ourselves.

Bosnia is not a big country. A typical mission would take about two hours. At the time, we were flying over only the northwest corner of the country. We knew from intelligence reports that there were missile batteries to the west, the north, and the northeast of our mission route. To keep away from them we flew a pattern called a combat air patrol. A CAP. It's like going around the oval of a racetrack. What we didn't know was that the enemy had been watching us fly that same pattern over and over again for more than a year.

This all started more than a year earlier, in February 1994, when we intercepted six Serbian aircraft in the no-fly zone. We watched them execute a bombing strike. We asked for permission to engage those planes, and we ended up shooting down five of them. It was the first military action ever taken by NATO.

So our repeated flying of that oval pattern was to ensure that no more enemy airstrikes occurred. Meanwhile, they knew who we were, who had shot down their planes, and they wanted revenge.

It was the middle of the afternoon on June 2, 1995, and we're flying our oval pattern over Bosnia. Suddenly my flight leader's warning system picks up what seems to be a radar lock from a missile battery. Well, we have other reconnaissance aircraft flying above us to double-check when that happens. And the word came back that they hadn't detected tracking radar emissions. We made our usual turn at the western end of our pattern and came back to the east. Now my warning system goes off. I looked around to see if we were being shot at. I learned later that two missiles had been fired at us. One passed between our two planes. The second one slammed into the belly of my plane, about ten feet behind where I was sitting.

These missiles are armed with exploding warheads. They shoot out metal shrapnel on impact, and this ignites the aircraft fuel and turns your own plane into a bomb.

My plane broke apart and the cockpit section where I was sitting sheared away as the plane burned. I was engulfed in flames before I could eject. I was looking straight down at the ground, spinning slowly to the left. I searched for the ejection handle, which was between my legs, and pulled. The first thing that happens is that the canopy blows off and rocket motors carry it away from the fuselage. If it doesn't separate properly—if the canopy is damaged—then the ejection seat won't fire and you're trapped in a flaming metal coffin as it falls to earth. Fortunately, my canopy exploded off cleanly. Milliseconds later the ejection seat fired and I was rocketed away from the plane.

You pull about twenty Gs as the seat accelerates. It's a kick in the pants. Of course it's much calmer than the missile impact and subsequent explosion, and there's a big feeling of relief to be clear of the plane. But in that same instant I was worried about what we call flailing injuries. These are what can happen to a pilot when he ejects at high speed and is suddenly subjected to a windblast in excess of 500 m.p.h. That windblast can break arms and legs and even kill you.

There was a lot of debris around me. I remember seeing a piece of the aircraft fly past. The windblast tore off pieces of my flight suit, including a patch with my name and my wings, which had been attached with Velcro. The visor of my helmet was gone. My face and neck had been burned and felt like they were still on fire. My mask felt like it was melting into my face and I ripped it off. Now I had no supplemental oxygen. It's also extremely cold. I'm at 27,000 feet, looking down at the ground and not knowing if my parachute is going to work or if it had been damaged in the explosion and fire. For all I knew, it was on fire right then.

And this is where your training saves you. You're not afraid. You're just reacting to the situation. You work through the emergency procedures for this problem step-by-step. We like to say that there are two types of ejections. There's the kind you can prepare for. You slow down, find a good place, and eject at an altitude that leaves you plenty of clearance above the ground but not so much that you'll be coming down under the chute forever. The other kind of ejection is the one you should have done two seconds earlier.

My situation was obviously the latter. I didn't make any decision about ejecting. It was instinct. But now I had to think. I didn't know if the ejection seat was damaged. I didn't know if the parachute would work. It was behind me, and I figured that pretty much everything that had been behind me in the plane had burned. Now I'm looking at the ground, five miles below, and thinking either the parachute opens or I fall to my death. I thought that if the parachute was on fire, maybe opening it would put the fire out. So I went ahead and manually deployed the parachute. And to my relief, I started slowing down. I'm now 25,000 feet in the air, but I'm floating under a canopy that turns out to be intact. Plus, I didn't suffer any flailing injuries. A broken ankle or leg would have ended any hope of avoiding capture once I hit the ground.

Your rate of descent after the chute opens is about one thousand feet per minute, so I knew it would be close to twenty-five minutes before I was on the ground. Somehow I didn't feel the lack of oxygen. I didn't feel cold. I have no explanation for either. Instead, I'm looking down and trying to match up the terrain with the area I knew I had been flying over. We knew there were no friendlies on the ground, no safe houses to hide in. We were over all-bad-guy territory on which three armies were fighting. I knew if I was caught it was likely I'd be shot on the spot and have my body dragged around in front of cameras to send a message to America that it should get out.

I could see villages and farmhouses. It was a populated area. I could also see a little armada of trucks and vehicles following along underneath me. Some of the people in those vehicles were later interviewed for a documentary and they admitted they planned to kill me as soon as they found me.

I'm under a plain, round parachute that simply drifts down—not the kind of rectangular chute that flies through the air and you can steer. It's like I've got a big sign over my head. They can see me and they know who I am. That's what happens when you get shot down in an airplane—you land right on top of the people who did it.

I got lucky. I landed away from a highway and near some trees where I could hide, but not *in* the trees where I would have been entangled and quickly discovered. I focused on making a good landing, because at this point the last thing I want to do is sprain an ankle and get caught.

As soon as I was down I grabbed my survival sack and ran about two hundred yards into the trees. I broke out my radio and tried to call my flight leader, but of course all I got was static. It had been a half hour since I'd been hit. Moments later I heard vehicles approaching and then I heard voices from where I ditched the parachute. I shut off the radio and crawled under some low-lying tree branches. An old man and a teenager walked by within six feet of me. They were the only people I'd see in the coming days who were not armed. Everybody else was in paramilitary gear and carrying SKS rifles.

It was about three thirty in the afternoon now. It wouldn't be dark for another six hours. Those were the longest six hours of my life. It was 7:00 p.m. when I heard the first gunshot. I could see paramilitary walking all around. Some were close and some farther off—but it was clear they were all looking for me. They weren't out hunting deer. They were shooting at anything that moved or made a noise that might be me. I counted a total of six shots. I stopped hoping that any of these people might be friendly.

A lot of stuff went through my mind as I lay there hiding. When the missile hit my plane I thought I was dead. I'd thought then about God. I'd put my belief and trust in Christ when I was a boy but had not been as committed to my faith as I should have. Yet I'd just survived a moment when I'd wondered what it was going to be like to step from life into death and then into the life that I believe comes after. You know how people react to news that they have a terminal illness—they go through a range of emotions that can include fear, denial, despair, anger, sadness. I'd just come through all of that in the span of a half hour. I told myself I couldn't afford emotions now. I had work to do if I was going to get out of this situation alive.

Your training gives you a foundation, a belief that you can overcome obstacles even when the odds are against you. I came up with a game plan. I made it my mission to get home safely. I made a mental list of what I had to do and I prioritized everything. Ultimately, though, your will to survive is the most important thing. In survival school you're taught to avoid wishful thinking or dwelling on the negative. None of that will help you. Instead you have to look for small victories and stay positive.

Of course, I had so much time to just stay still and think that some negative thoughts were unavoidable. I thought about the paramilitaries who were searching for me and how they shot off their weapons. Maybe the next bullet would be the one that goes through my head. Maybe I'd be buried right there, in an unmarked grave. I thought how sad it would be if I died without ever having married and had kids.

These kinds of thoughts would pass through my mind quickly—and then it was back to the work of survival. Two things I was careful about were minimizing my movements and trying not to make any sound. You try to break that down, to be camouflaged, to not give up your outline but instead blend in with your surroundings. You have to stay still. Motion attracts attention. Noise carries a long way. That first night I waited a long time, until it was fully dark. Then I spent two hours crawling out from my hiding place and only about three feet into the grass. I kept on slowly. This is the essence of evasion. Whether you're moving or stationary, you try to be invisible.

When I got to an area away from where I'd come down and I felt more secure, I inventoried my survival gear. Then I started to plan for the worst-case scenario. How long could I last with what I had? I didn't have any food, not much water. The battery in my radio, which was critical, would be good for about fifteen hours, so I knew I could use it only in short intervals. I figured that if I could find food and was careful with the radio, I could make it forty-five days. Not that I would have given up and died at that point. I planned to do whatever it would take, even if I had to walk out more than eighty miles over a mountain range to reach the coast.

In the end, of course, I was only there six days—from June 2 to June 8. I hid in three different locations. I became nocturnal. I moved only at night, and only when I felt I needed to evade capture. I had a handheld GPS unit and a compass, but they would illuminate at night and threatened to give away my location, so I used them sparingly after dark. Mostly I used the stars to find my way. My nights became my days and my days became my nights. During the days I never napped for more than twenty minutes. I had to stay alert because there were people everywhere looking for me. And there was always the chance that somebody who wasn't looking for me would find me by accident. One time a farmer brought his cows into a field where I was hiding and I could hear him very close by.

I couldn't risk building a fire, so I got cold and wet and felt hypothermic all the time. I didn't have much water, just a couple of small packages. You're trained not to ration your water. Instead you ration your sweat by keeping your exertion to a minimum. But my heart pounded like I was running a marathon, day and night. I ended up losing more than twenty-five pounds in those six days. Water was my primary concern. If you're dehydrated you make poor decisions, and that could get me killed—a situation I regarded as unfavorable. I had a map, but it wasn't detailed enough for me to find a water source. I listened for the trickle of a stream, tried to watch out for any animal activity that might indicate water nearby. There was a farmhouse nearby, but I wasn't desperate enough yet to take that chance. Sometimes it would drizzle in the afternoon and one day it rained fairly hard. I had a little sponge, and I used it to collect rain droplets off leaves. I'd squeeze it out into a Ziploc bag.

On one of my last days I couldn't feel my feet because they were so cold and wet. It's a condition called immersion foot. They were shriveled and there was no blood going to my toes, so I knew the nerve endings were dying. I took off my boots, which were plain leather and not waterproof, and took off my socks to try to warm up my feet. The socks were wet, so I wrung them out into my Ziploc. I only got a few drops—not enough to drink, but just enough to put some moisture onto my swollen, dried-out lips. It tasted terrible, but I treated it like a small victory, one more positive step toward surviving.

At night I'd sometimes get disoriented, especially in the trees. I had to stay away from open fields because many of them were mined. I'd wait until after midnight to move and then try to find a good hiding place to bed down in by 5:00 a.m. My survival training really paid off.

The map I had in my survival kit had some information about local plants, but I didn't have much time to read up on them. I ate some leaves and some grass that I grabbed as I went along. I knew from my training that insects are high in protein and good to eat. So are worms. I ended up eating some ants. It turned out to be more of a form of entertainment, a little mental break from the tension. They were crunchy and tasted like lemon.

I kept moving to the south, because there was high terrain in that direction. That's where my radio would work better, because it was a line-of-sight device. It wasn't a satellite phone or a cell phone—just a radio that could talk to airplanes. I tried to make contact every hour, and I listened to my frequencies to see if anybody was trying to contact me. I'd call out, "Anyone, Basher Five Two," hoping somebody would hear me. I didn't hear anything back until the third night, when I heard a faint, broken transmission. But I wasn't able to establish contact with that aircraft.

The next night I was on higher ground but still didn't hear anything back when I sent out a call. But then on the fifth night I made contact with a friend of mine, Captain Thomas Hanford. He was in an F-16 over the ocean about eighty miles from my position. It was late. Hanford had stayed out past his return time after asking permission to look for me on the radio. He had about a half hour of fuel onboard. He pushed closer to the coast to get a better angle of transmission into the valleys where I might be. He didn't know if I was still alive, but he wouldn't give up. I'll be in his debt for as long as I live. He kept on calling in the blind, "Basher One One for Basher Five Two. Basher One One for Basher Five Two."

I was on a hillside, listening to my frequencies and calling out, sending out my beacon. I heard three metallic clicks. Then I heard a broken transmission. Suddenly I heard clearly, "Basher One One for Basher Five Two." I wanted to scream. I cupped my hand around the radio and whispered back, "Basher Five Two. Basher Five Two." And he answered, "Copy that." Then he asked me what squadron I'd served with in Korea to make sure it was me, and not somebody who'd picked up my radio after I was shot down. I gave him the right answer and said, "I'm alive."

When he said it was good to hear my voice it was a moment I'll never forget, a flood of emotions. I wanted to cry, I wanted to laugh. I wanted to scream and jump for joy. I had to control all that. I reminded myself I was a soldier with a job to do. And just because I'd made radio contact didn't mean I was home safe. But after that everything happened fast. The NATO supreme commander, Admiral Leighton Smith, asked the Marines on board the USS *Kearsarge*, which was nearest to my position, if they could pull off a daytime rescue. Normally we prefer to make rescues at night, because the cover of darkness is an advantage with our night vision capabilities. But Admiral Smith was worried about giving enemy forces on the ground time to set up an ambush. He wanted to go immediately and they did—two attack helicopters, two troop-carrying helicopters with Marines onboard, and support fighters overhead. These were all aircraft that were already to go that day. They just needed a mission, and no mission is more satisfying than saving one of our own.

I sent out my location using two different codes and identifying myself with personal information that was on my intelligence card so they'd know it was me and not a trap. F-18s came over to check the coordinates I'd given. Then, as I heard the helicopters coming in, I reported the position of small arms fire I had heard the day before. I was also giving them headings that would fly them in to my position. The sound of the helicopters kept getting louder until finally I saw one of them cresting the horizon. I'm a patriotic guy all the time, but at that moment, seeing my country coming for me in hostile territory, I was as proud to be an American as I've ever been.

The helicopters circled my position. It was getting light. There was a fog lifting, and the pilots could make out houses in the distance. There wasn't a clear landing area, but they set down anyway, practically standing on their tails to get down between the trees. One landed on obstructions that prevented the rear door from opening so the Marines could deploy. Marines from the other helicopter did get out and set up a rough perimeter. They told me to run to the nearest helicopter as quickly as I could. Nobody was shooting at them yet, but they wanted to spend as little time on the ground as possible.

I made it onboard a helicopter and we took off. On the egress we were shot at with shoulder-fired missiles. A couple of them passed close by. Then a large gun emplacement started shooting at us. The door gunner returned fire, but our mission was to get out of there, not to stay and fight. There was also a lot of small arms fire directed at us. One round entered the tail section of the helicopter I was in. It ricocheted and slammed into a sergeant major sitting across from me. But it hit his canteen, fell on the floor, and rolled up against the boot of another Marine. He picked it up, looked at it for a second, and put it in his pocket.

Ever since I was twelve years old, I wanted to be a pilot, a great pilot. It was not only a priority but it was my entire life. But six days alone in Bosnia changed everything for me.

With all that time isolated, hiding in the grass, I had time to think. My years of training saved my life—that was for sure. But when you think your life could be over any minute, you ask a lot of questions. Have I been a good person? Were my priorities in the right place? Since I was a young boy, I had not given those questions or my faith much thought. In many ways, my life had been all about me. But it didn't take long for me to know that had to change. Years later, after much soul searching and asking myself questions, I entered and graduated from the Dallas Theological Seminary.

COLIN POWELL

It's become known over the years that if you're looking for General Colin Powell on a weekend, you might check the garage. He loves cars. His love of cars started when he and his wife, Alma, bought a new 1961 Volkswagen Beetle while they were stationed in Germany. Since then, General Powell has fallen in love with vintage. He has restored over twenty Volvos from the 1950s and '60s, which he then sells—not so much for the money, but for the opportunity to take on yet another restoration job, yet another car.

The defining moments and influences that Colin shared may really resonate with you. They did for me. No matter how far we travel or how long we are gone, our lives can be richer and stronger when we have a place in our hearts we can think of as "home."

I owe whatever success I've had to a place called Banana Kelly. But first things first. My parents immigrated to the United States from Jamaica in the 1920s. My father, Luther Powell, arrived in 1920 at the Port of Philadelphia. My mother, Maud McKoy, came through Ellis Island in 1924. Like so many millions before them, they came for economic reasons.

My father lived in different parts of New York City for several years before renting a room in a large Harlem apartment. He was immediately smitten with the landlady's daughter—and the feelings were mutual. So he not only got a room, he found a wife. In the early years of their marriage, Luther and Maud stayed in Harlem, which is where my sister, Marilyn, and I were born.

My mother was a high school graduate, and my father wasn't. Whenever they had an argument, she would mumble under her breath, "He, who never graduated from high school." They were both fun loving—everyone in the family was. It's a West Indian approach to life, full of music and laughter. My mother was a great cook who developed her own Jamaican American cuisine. She would use traditional Jamaican spices on American dishes like hamburgers, but we also ate a lot of plantain, rice and peas, and roasted goat.

There was always rum in the house. My father enjoyed an evening highball of rum and ginger ale, a family tradition I've tried to maintain. My mother only drank on holidays or celebrations. She would demurely ask for "a touch of rum," by which she meant a big slug of rum with a splash of ginger ale.

When I was two, we moved to a better neighborhood. In our case it was to Fox Street and then to Kelly Street in the South Bronx. Years later, the area developed a terrible reputation, but in the 1930s it was beautiful, with wide boulevards lined with apartment houses and side streets filled with modest, tidy houses.

We called our four-block corner of the neighborhood Banana Kelly, because the street was curved like one. Lots of our extended family lived in Banana Kelly. All the parents felt responsibility for all the cousins; it was like a pride of lions watching over their cubs.

Banana Kelly was a great, nurturing place to grow up. It was diverse and filled with hardworking, caring people. I had lots of friends, and after school we played stickball in the street until we heard our mothers call out "Dinner!" Even with families that weren't related, there was a sense of people looking out for each other.

Economically, everyone was on the same level. My dad made about $60 a week. Because both my parents worked, I got a new Schwinn bicycle, and eventually we got a car. That was a big day in the Powell household.

I went to the local public school. In the late 1940s and early 1950s, New York's public school system was strong. The teachers, who taught hard but fair, remain some of my great heroes. It was among the few truly integrated institutions in the country. And we all got along. In fact, we kidded each other about our ethnicity in ways that would get you in trouble today.

Banana Kelly defined my childhood. At the end of one block was Thomas J. Knowlton Junior High School. We lived at the other end. As I walked to school, cousins and friends would join me, their mothers watching from the windows. As we approached Knowlton, we passed St. Margaret's Episcopal Church, which was a major part of our family life; it provided community, support, and a call to be our best in everything we did.

In addition to the Jamaican *patois* I learned at home, I picked up some Yiddish from my Jewish friends and some Spanish from my Puerto Rican friends. There were also lots of Italians in the neighborhood. Sammy Fiorino was the shoemaker; he was able to extend a pair of shoes way past their expected lifespan. Sammy taught me how to play poker. We'd play right in the store, usually with a couple of off-duty cops. One evening, a rookie cop came in and said he was going to have to break up our game. The two veterans took him outside for a little chat. We were never disturbed again.

All in all, the neighborhood was a colorful, enriching mix. I was exposed to different cultures and languages. I *know* Americans can all get along—because I lived it.

As a teenager, my world expanded. I could get on the subway and visit any neighborhood I wanted. Between my Schwinn and the subway system, I was wandering all over New York City by the time I was thirteen.

In 1950, when I was getting ready to finish Knowlton Junior High, I went to see my guidance counselor. Even though my grades were mediocre, I told him I wanted to apply to Stuyvesant or Bronx High School of Science, the city's top public schools.

Jump ahead forty years to when I was working on my memoirs. I wrote to the New York City Board of Education asking if they had any records of my school career. Well, they had everything—every single report card from kindergarten through City College. Included in all the papers was a note written by that guidance counselor: "Young Powell wants to apply to the Bronx High School of Science; we advised against it."

And so I went to Morris High School, our local school. And I received a terrific education there, although I can't say my grades improved dramatically. I also had a great time. I ran track, the only thing I was any good at athletically.

Between classes, the track team, part-time jobs, and church activities, my high school years were busy. I was a junior sexton at church—I used to carry the cross, and on important days such as Christmas and Easter, I would chant the epistle of the day. My mother considered it a great honor to see her son up there, all decked out in robes and whatnot, chanting away.

There were no prayers allowed in school. Every religion you could imagine was represented in the student body at Morris, and on Tuesday afternoon we had something called "religious convocation." If you were Jewish, you would go to temple and study the Torah. If you were Catholic, you went to catechism classes. And if you were Episcopalian, you went home. That's how faith was expressed without crossing the line between church and state.

Now that I'm in my seventies, I find myself reflecting back on my childhood. I remember the exposure to arts and music that I got at public school. At the time, it probably bored me to death, but the arts can work their magic even if we resist them at first. I remember Ravel's *Boléro*, Chaucer's *The Canterbury Tales*, Rembrandt's *The Night Watch*. I'm a big proponent of arts education; I believe it humanizes us.

One day when I was fourteen, a man named Jay Sickser, who owned a toy and children's furniture store in the neighborhood, stopped me on the street. He said, "Hey, kid, would you like to do some work?" I said, "Yeah." I spent that first day unloading a truck. When I was finished, he said, "You're a good worker. Why don't you come back tomorrow?" I did, and again the day after that. I worked on and off for Mr. Sickser, who was a Russian Jewish immigrant, for the next seven or eight years until I graduated from college and joined the army. The whole Sickser family pitched in at the store. They were flexible about my hours, but I always made sure I was available to help them during the Christmas rush.

One day, after I'd been working in the store for a couple of years, Mr. Sickser asked me to step into the back room. He said, "Colin, you're a good worker, a good kid, and I love your family. But I don't want you to think that there's any future for you here in this store. It will go to my daughter and son-in-law. You need to get your education and keep moving." I thanked him for that, and I've never forgotten it. Of course, I didn't plan on spending the rest of my life loading and unloading baby furniture, but I was deeply touched that he would say that to me.

Time passed, and the neighborhood deteriorated. Jay Sickser's store closed, he died, his wife died, his daughter died, his son-in-law, Lou Kirchner, sold everything, retired to Florida, and remarried. Then one day he opened the newspaper and saw that I'd been named national security advisor to President Reagan. He was so excited, saying to his wife, "Oh my God, look at this! Little Colin Powell from back in the Bronx! I made this kid what he is today!" He just took unbridled delight in my success. When I became chairman of the Joint Chiefs of Staff, he and his wife visited me at the Pentagon. And for the remaining years of his life, whenever I was in Florida, they'd come to my hotel and we'd have a chat in the lobby. He'd wave over strangers, saying, "Come and meet my friend Colin Powell."

People often ask me if I dreamed about becoming a general or even secretary of state when I was a kid. I smile and jokingly say, "Of course I did. There I was, ten years old, standing on the corner of

163rd and Kelly and saying to myself, 'Self, you are going to grow up and become chairman of the Joint Chiefs of Staff.'" It was unthinkable—a working-class black kid from the South Bronx in the 1940s.

What did happen was that I went to City College of New York, even though my grades were a little below their standard for admission. Maybe it was because I was black or because they felt sorry for me or because they liked the essay I wrote for admission. I also got into New York University, but I chose CCNY because it was free. NYU cost $750 a year.

My mom wanted me to study engineering, but engineering and I didn't agree with each other. I switched to geology because it was the easiest route to a degree. Then one day I discovered ROTC. I loved the discipline, the order, and the uniform, which gave me some longed-for status. I also met some great guys, many of whom became lifelong friends. ROTC changed my life.

Four and a half years later, with my BS in geology, I was commissioned as a second lieutenant of infantry in the US Army, and my career began. I had no idea where it would lead. When people asked me what my ambition was, I would answer, "Just to be a good soldier every day and to see what comes along." The army never made me any promises, but we were a good fit from the start.

My parents wanted me to return to civilian life. In fact, they wondered where they'd gone wrong. But I stuck with it, and before long I'd done a tour in Germany and two in Vietnam. I'd also met and married my wife, Alma. But the family still wanted me to quit. Alma and I had dinner one night with my Aunt Laurice, who was the matriarch of the family. She immediately started bugging me about getting out of the army. Finally I said, "I'll be eligible for a lifetime pension when I'm forty-one." That was the end of the discussion, because my family—like so many immigrant families—was all about achieving financial security. If you could get a good pension at age forty-one, that was a good job. The fact that you could get killed in the process was kind of secondary.

Of course, after I was promoted to brigadier general, all I heard from my mother was, "My son, the general." I wish Dad could have seen it, but he had died two years earlier.

It was CCNY that gave me a quality education that allowed me to hold my own with fellow officers who had graduated from West Point, Harvard, Princeton, the Virginia Military Academy, and Texas A&M. We were a band of brothers; the only thing that mattered was performance and results. I worked hard, stayed out of trouble, tried to be as good a soldier as I could be, and let the future and destiny take its course.

In 1997, the Rudin family, among the city's most dedicated philan-thropists, contacted me to say they wanted to create a public policy center at City College in my name. Of course, I was honored and agreed.

In the ensuing years, I was busy and unable to devote a lot of time to the Powell Center for Policy Studies. When I left the State Depart-ment at the beginning of 2005, my schedule opened up. I went up to the campus and met with about a dozen students at the center. They were all immigrants from low-income families, and they all had come to CCNY pretty much like I had fifty years earlier.

The focus of the center was on teaching these young men and women how to be leaders by exposing them to the business commu-nity and linking their academic work to real-world experience in the community. We call it service-learning. So if students are studying health care, they find a volunteer position at a hospital or health center. This takes learning out of the realm of theory and emphasizes results, on what works on the ground.

The Powell Center grew into a much larger Colin Powell School for Civic and Global Leadership, which was inaugurated on May 2, 2013. It was a tremendously moving ceremony for me. Some of our students spoke, including Lev Sviridov, an immigrant from Russia who is only the second Rhodes Scholar in City University of New York history. Then there was Trevor Houser, an Oregon high school dropout with a criminal record. He wandered across the country, showed up in New York, and decided he wanted to do something with his life. So he earned his GED, got into CCNY, and did brilliantly. Now he's a China specialist, working in that country and doing great things in energy and the environment.

As I mentioned earlier, the South Bronx fell on hard times. It became a national symbol for urban decay. Jobs left New York City; the whole garment industry, for example, moved overseas in pursuit of cheap labor. With little economic opportunity, people lost hope. Drugs came in. Banana Kelly turned into a war zone. The house I grew up in was burned to its shell. Then the junkies stole the copper piping. It was block after block of skeleton houses. I would take my children there when they were young because I wanted them to understand their heritage. They witnessed the deterioration.

One of the proudest moments of my life happened in the fall of 2010. A new apartment building was built about two blocks from where I grew up. It's a beautiful building, constructed to the highest green standards, with a garden on the roof and energy-efficient systems. I went to the dedication. I suppose I should mention the building is called the Colin Powell Apartments. It gave me hope.

As a native New Yorker, the renewal of my hometown has been gratifying to see. To my surprise and delight, my daughters moved to the city to pursue their careers. I, of course, left to pursue mine. But my gratitude and connection to Banana Kelley have never wavered. It was a nurturing and inspirational place to start a life.

ROBERT REICH

When young Robert Reich headed to Oxford to be a Rhodes Scholar, he decided to take a ship across the Atlantic rather than fly. Not long onboard, Reich got seasick and was confined to his cabin. The first night in his cabin, there came a knock at the door. "Hi, I'm Bill Clinton. I heard you were sick and thought maybe this would help." He handed Reich a bowl of chicken soup and crackers. Clinton, too, was on his way to Oxford and although they had met briefly before boarding the ship, this was their first real contact—and the beginning of a lifelong friendship.

The powerful influence in Bob's life shines a light on childhood experiences—in his case being bullied. We are all shaped in one way or another by our childhood relationships and while we may think we have grown beyond them, they often, sometimes dramatically, influence us well into adulthood.

I am four feet eleven inches tall and have always been short. Starting in kindergarten, I was teased about my height. I remember being called names and being shoved around in the boys' bathroom. As a result I felt vulnerable. Early on, I developed a coping strategy: I latched onto an older, bigger boy and made him my protector.

When I was in kindergarten, I knew a boy who was in the fourth grade; his parents and mine were friends. I asked him if he would watch out for me. He said he would. I made sure we were seen together in the hallways and on the playground. The bullies got the message and backed off.

Growing up, I spent part of every summer at my grandmother's house in the foothills of New York's Adirondack Mountains. The bullying continued there. I met an older boy in the neighborhood who had kind eyes and a warm smile. I befriended him, and he made sure that no one messed with me. That boy's name was Michael "Mickey" Schwerner and, although neither one of us could have suspected it at the time, he changed my life.

I was born in Scranton, Pennsylvania, in 1946. My father was in the women's clothing business. When I was six, we moved to northern Westchester County, to what was, in the 1950s, a small farming town. Today it's an upscale New York suburb, but back then it was largely working class. My father opened two moderately priced stores.

I never felt deprived, but money was always a concern. I remember my father coming home from work and worrying about not being able to pay the bills. My mother stayed home until the mid-fifties, and then she joined my father in running the stores.

In the late fifties, my parents realized that wealth was moving north in Westchester. They responded by taking their stores upscale, and they did well. While they certainly never became rich, I was happy to see my father relax as his financial insecurity lessened.

My parents were not political; they were too busy making a living. My father was a Republican, my mother a Democrat. We almost never talked politics. I remember, though, watching the McCarthy hearings with my father and him calling Joe McCarthy a son of a bitch. I was vaguely aware that McCarthy was hurting people and abusing his authority, and I certainly recognized his bullying demeanor and tactics from my own experience. When Edward R. Murrow went public with his concerns about the McCarthy witch hunts, my father cheered him on. But generally, the great issues of the day didn't concern me.

I graduated from high school in 1964 and entered Dartmouth that fall. I'd heard about three young civil rights workers—two white and one black—who disappeared in Neshoba County, Mississippi, in June, but their bodies weren't discovered until months later. One of them was Mickey Schwerner, my childhood protector. I had lost track of Mickey. He had originally attended Michigan State and wanted to be a veterinarian but had since transferred to Columbia to major in social work. Mickey had gotten married, and he had dedicated himself to fighting for social justice and equality. He had headed off to Mississippi where the action was. I was horrified and deeply shaken by the news of his death. The local sheriff had engineered the murder, and the injustice and sheer savagery of the crime was staggering.

The impact of Mickey's death dramatically changed my life. For the first time, I took a good look at the world around me. I began to take an active interest in the civil rights movement. That led me to the anti-Vietnam War movement, which was just beginning. I got involved in campus politics and was elected president of my freshman, sophomore, and junior classes.

I went to Washington at the end of my junior year and spent the summer interning for Senator Robert Kennedy. Kennedy cared deeply about the poor, and I worked on antipoverty initiatives in his office. I took time off during my senior year to work for Gene McCarthy's presidential campaign because I was convinced that the Vietnam War was wrongheaded, dangerous, and diverting the nation's attention and resources away from pressing domestic needs.

The following year, both Martin Luther King Jr. and Robert Kennedy were assassinated. There was rioting in our cities, and the Vietnam conflict was escalating. Like millions of others of my generation, I couldn't stand on the sidelines. My commitment to public service took firm hold, eventually leading to my being appointed secretary of labor by Bill Clinton.

Today, my youthful optimism has been tempered by time and experience, but my students where I now teach at the University of California, Berkeley, renew it and give me hope. Mickey Schwerner was just twenty-four when he was murdered working to make America a better place, a country that lives up to its ideal of liberty and justice for all. When I was a vulnerable child, Mickey protected me from harm. I, in turn, feel a responsibility to protect others. I was honored to know him, and I hope, in some small way, that my life's work honors his idealism, his courage, and his sacrifice.

MARY LOU RETTON

The first athlete to appear on the back of a Wheaties box was Lou Gehrig, the great New York Yankees baseball player, in 1934. Bob Richards, the decathlon gold medalist, became the first male athlete to appear on the front of the box. Not until twenty-six years later, in 1984, did Mary Lou Retton, who stands four foot nine, become the first female athlete to appear on the front of the Wheaties box.

I have thought often of the early moments that defined Mary Lou's life, not just because they are of unparalleled accomplishment, but because my father grew up in the poorest of mining towns in West Virginia, and I know how difficult that life can be. For anyone who started out life with the odds against them, it is what makes this tale of hard work, determination, and competitive spirit so astounding.

I was born and raised in the small coal-mining town of Fairmont, West Virginia. My father, Ron, worked in the coal-equipment business. My mother, Lois, was a homemaker. I was the youngest of five children, three boys and two girls. We were a tight-knit Italian American family. We were also very competitive.

I fit right in because I was born competitive. In addition, I was always small, and that caused me to overcompensate. My message to the family, neighborhood, and world: don't let my size fool you—I can do anything I set my mind to.

My brothers played baseball, basketball, and football. Back then there were few opportunities for girls to play sports, so my sister and I took tap and jazz classes at a local dance studio. They also offered ballet, but one lesson was enough for me—the frilly outfits and pointed toes were not my thing.

There was one class at the studio that I loved. The teacher laid out mats and we performed somersaults and cartwheels. It was called acrobatics and I took to it immediately. At home I was always getting in trouble for jumping around on Mom's bed, doing flips, and cart-wheeling down the hall. What earned me punishment at home won me praise in acrobatics class.

One of my most vivid childhood memories is of watching the 1976 Montreal Olympics. I was seven years old, and I was glued to the television. There was this little girl, Nadia Comaneci, and she was from this country called Romania. Nadia was doing these amazing things with her body, and there was a name for it: gymnastics. Sitting in our den in front of that TV I realized, "That's what I want to do!"

My sister Shari and I begged Mom to find us a gymnastics class, and she did. It was just thirty minutes down the interstate at West Virginia University, and taught by a man named Pete Longdon. Working with Pete, I quickly realized that being small and compact helps in gymnastics. It makes it easier to do flips, twists, and somer-saults. I was also very strong and had what Pete called "explosive" power and energy.

In 1977, Pete opened up a gymnastics center in Fairmont called Aerial Port. Gary Rafaloski was the assistant at the center, and he became my first serious coach. Gary worked with me for hours a day, nurtured me, and took whatever natural talents I had to the next level.

Between classes, I practiced for hours; they flew by because I loved what I was doing. I slept in my leotard so I'd be all ready to work out the next morning. I entered any and every competition I could, and by the time I was twelve, I was travelling around the country to meets.

I was fourteen years old and competing at a meet in Reno, Nevada, in December 1982, and Béla Károlyi was there. Béla was a legend because he'd been Nadia Comaneci's coach. He had defected to the United States just months earlier. He approached me in the middle of the competition, tapped me on the shoulder, and introduced himself. I was completely starstruck—the man was the king of gymnastics. He said, "Mary Lou, you come to me and I make you Olympic champion." I looked around for another short gymnast named Mary Lou—there was no way Béla Károlyi could be interested in me.

But he was. My parents happened to be at this meet, and he sat them down and said, "Mr. and Mrs. Retton, I think your daughter has what it takes. I'd like her to move to Houston for training with me."

My parents and I went back to Fairmont and considered Béla's offer. Actually we discussed it for hours, and then my parents left the decision up to me. I think we all knew it was a foregone conclusion. I told them, "I want to give this a shot." Looking back, I can hardly believe I was only fourteen. I packed for the move to Houston to train under Béla and his wife, Márta Károlyi.

I was excited and honored but also scared to death. I had never been away from home before, and I was going to be living with a family I'd never met, training with girls I didn't know in a very competitive gym. I was a big deal in West Virginia. In Houston I was nobody. When I got there, I kept a low profile and focused on the work.

My first big meet was the 1983 American Cup in Madison Square Garden in New York City. I'd only been working with Béla for two and a half months. In the world of international gymnastics, I was unknown. If I was noticed, I was dismissed as little hillbilly Mary Lou from West Virginia. I wasn't even there as a member of the team. I was an alternate, which means you step in if there's an injury. The night before the competition, one of the top girls pulled a muscle in her hip. It wasn't immediately clear if the injury would keep her out of the competition, and we all went back to our hotel.

About an hour later there was a knock on my door, and then I heard Béla's voice, "Mary Lou, it is me." He sat me in a chair and then sat facing me, our knees touching. Béla has mesmerizing eyes, and he looked at me and said, "Mary Lou, you will be competing tomorrow. This is your chance. Don't let me down." I nodded my head, but inside I was going, "*Alllll*-right! Ten weeks ago I was in the hills of West Virginia, and tomorrow I'm going to be competing in Madison Square Garden!"

After Béla left, the doubts kicked in. I thought, "Oh my God, I can't do this. There's no way I can do this. I'm not prepared." But I said to myself, "You know what, you have nothing to lose. You're a last-minute substitute who nobody knows or expects anything from, so if you mess up no one will notice."

The next day I took the floor at the Garden. The vault and floor exercises were always my best events. I started on vault, and I stuck my landing—which means your feet just glue to the mat; you don't hop, skip, or shuffle. The judges awarded me a 10. Then I did well on the parallel bars and earned a 9.8. The balance beam was next. It was my problem event, and I hadn't been with the Károlyis long enough for them to make me what we call "a beamer," even though I worked twice as hard on that event as I did on any other. But that day I nailed the balance beam. That was when I knew I had won the 1983 American Cup.

After that, my life got really intense. Everything took a backseat to training. Preparing for the Olympics is actually a very selfish pursuit. It's eight hours a day in the gym, and the rest of the time you're resting and taking care of your body so you can train, train, and train some more.

The Olympic trials were in Jacksonville, Florida, in June 1984. I placed first, securing a spot on the team. We flew back to Houston; the games were due to start in six weeks. I had my ticket to Los Angeles in my gym bag. The dream I'd had since I was a seven-year-old watching Nadia Comaneci was about to come true. I had worked hard, left home and school, and sacrificed a social life. It was all about to pay off.

Then disaster.

My right knee had been bothering me for a while, but I didn't think much about it because as an athlete you're trained to suck it up. And Béla had little patience for injuries: "Tape it up, ice it, don't complain." The day after we got back to Houston from the trials I trained for eight hours, well into the evening. I was doing one final floor routine and was in midair on the last tumbling pass when I heard and felt my knee pop. I finished the routine, then sat down on the corner of the mat to catch my breath. When I went to stand up, I couldn't. My knee had started to swell. Something was very wrong.

Béla was across the gym. I managed to stand, hobble over to him, and say, with tears in my eyes, "I can't straighten my knee, it's locked."

Béla said, "Whachu mean!" It was almost as if he was offended.

"I can't straighten my knee, I don't know what's wrong, I heard it pop." I was getting desperate.

"Go home, you sleep with ice on it, you be here at 7:00 a.m. for workout."

So I went back to the hotel, put an enormous ice pack on my knee, and went to bed. In the morning, my knee was the size of a soccer ball, and I was rushed to the emergency room. They did a bunch of tests and found ligament and cartilage damage. I needed surgery. Our team doctors said there was no way I'd be able to compete in Los Angeles, telling me I'd need to keep the knee immobile for six weeks after surgery before I could start training again.

Everyone told me to go back home to West Virginia and wait for the 1988 Olympics, that it just wasn't my time. I was dejected: "Oh, why me? Why did this have to happen?" But within minutes I snapped back, refocused, and said to myself, "Who's going to tell me what I can or can't do? I've made it this far. I'm not going to let them put a limit on me."

I flew to Richmond, Virginia, where one of the best arthroscopic surgeons in the country performed the surgery. I flew back to Houston and the next day I was back in the gym with a big brace on my knee. The uneven bars put far less stress on the knees, so I concentrated on them at first. Two weeks later I was doing two workouts a day. When we arrived in Los Angeles, I was ready to compete.

The opening ceremony, with athletes from almost every nation in the world present, was stirring. Because we were the host country, we were the last team to enter the stadium. And since we gymnasts were the smallest athletes on the American team, we were in front. Marching into the Coliseum behind the flag, hearing the crowd cheer, looking out at thousands of happy faces, was a living, walking, soon-to-be flipping and flying dream.

For me, the most memorable moment of the games was when I landed my vault dismount. The judges gave me a 10, and I knew I had won the gold medal. I ran into Béla's arms, and he lifted me high above his head and said, "You are the Olympic champion." I won five medals in all, including the first all-around gold ever won by an American woman.

Since the Olympics, I've gotten married to my husband, Shannon Kelley, had four daughters, written two books, appeared in several movies, and even had my own television show.

Looking back, it has been a wonderful, full life, for which I am deeply grateful. Sometimes I look back at that little seven-year-old in, of all places, Fairmont, West Virginia, glued to her television set watching the Olympics, and I have to smile. Those fast eight years of training, and even the trauma with my knee, were the greatest influence on my life. They taught me a lot about myself. When I am told, "No, you can't," I am determined to prove them wrong.

CONDOLEEZZA RICE

Many in Washington know that Condi Rice planned early in life to pursue a career in music. An excellent pianist, she first played on stage at the age of fifteen with the Denver Symphony. She has since played at numerous public and diplomatic events, including for Queen Elizabeth II, and performed with such great musicians as cellist Yo-Yo Ma. Many historians will tell you that Thomas Jefferson, who played the violin, was the only other secretary of state to be as talented a musician.

As previous stories in the book reveal, there are any number of powerful influences and defining moments that can change our lives. Condi's story reminds us that some lives are changed by events that occur even before we are born.

A set of books purchased a hundred years ago changed my life. My paternal great-grandmother, Julia Head, was a slave. She was born on a cotton plantation in Green County, Alabama, and, according to family lore, she was favored in the household and was taught to read. She was freed after the Civil War, when she was thirteen. She married a sharecropper, and, in 1892, she gave birth to my grandfather, John Wesley Rice. He was a bright, curious child, and Julia taught him to read at an early age. Growing up, he loved learning and was determined to go to college.

John was admitted to Stillman College in Tuscaloosa, Alabama. Stillman was founded by Presbyterians in 1875; its original mission was "the training of colored men for the ministry." In the days before he went there, Grandfather Rice spent many hours picking cotton, but he only earned enough to cover his freshman tuition. The school told him he couldn't return for his sophomore year. They also told him that if he agreed to study for the ministry he would be eligible for a scholarship. That's how my grandfather became a Presbyterian minister.

After graduation, John met my grandmother, who was from Baton Rouge and was half Creole. They were a dynamic couple who founded several schools and churches in Alabama and Mississippi before settling in Louisiana, where my father and his sister were born.

The Rice family was dedicated to education. My father vividly remembered the day, during the Great Depression, when my grandfather came home with nine leather-bound, gold-embossed books. They were the works of Victor Hugo, William Shakespeare, and other literary giants. My grandmother asked him how much he'd paid for them. When he answered ninety dollars—a huge sum at the time—she told him to take them back. He said he'd arranged to pay for them on time. She still insisted he return them. Despite the drama, the books stayed. My grandfather believed in having books in the home, and, more importantly, he believed in having his children read them.

When I received my PhD, my father, John, gave me the five remaining books. Today they sit on my mantelpiece. My grandfather died just before I was born, but he has inspired me all my life. Whenever I look at those books, I feel his legacy. It's a profound connection; he was definitely the intellectual guide of the family.

When my grandfather died, my father took over as pastor at his church in Birmingham. He'd earned a BA in history and a master's in theology and didn't really want to be a pastor, but felt obligated. It was a part-time job—he also taught school. He later earned a second master's in education and ended his career as vice chancellor at Denver University. His sister, my Aunt Theresa, earned a PhD in Victorian literature at the University of Wisconsin; she went on to write a book about Charles Dickens. Given this history, there is nothing surprising about the fact that I went to college and got a doctorate.

My mother's side of the family was not as well educated. They lived in southeastern Alabama and were fair skinned; my maternal great-grandfather was white. When my grandfather, Albert Ray, was thirteen, he beat up a white man who had assaulted his sister. Fearing for his life, he ran away from home and made his way to Birmingham. At the train station there, he was befriended by a white man named Mr. Wheeler, who brought him into his household. The Wheelers were mine owners, and my grandfather learned construction and blacksmithing in their businesses. He worked in the coal mines during the day and as a blacksmith in the evenings and built houses on weekends. He made a good living.

My maternal grandmother was the daughter of a bishop of the African Methodist Episcopal Church. She was raised in a patrician manner in Birmingham. I have a picture of her at finishing school, taken when she was sixteen; she's wearing pearls and a lace dress. She went on to study piano, and, while my grandfather was working his many jobs, she gave piano lessons to local children out of their home.

They had five children, including my mother, Angelena. My mother went to Miles College, a historically black college in Birmingham. She went on to become a high school science, music, and oratory teacher. She met my father when they taught at the same public school. Music was a major influence in her life; she came up with my given name from an Italian musical term *con dolcezza*, which means "with sweetness."

My parents married on Valentine's Day 1954, and I came along exactly nine months later. My mother always joked that it was a good thing I didn't arrive early.

In addition to being an educator, my father was an athlete. He also loved history and politics. He became a Republican because we lived under Jim Crow laws that were enacted and enforced by the Democrats who controlled Alabama politics at the time. My father's temperament was pragmatic; my mother's more artistic.

My parents started me on French, figure skating, and ballet lessons when I was three. I began studying piano because my parents would leave me with my grandmother while they were at work. I would watch her students come and go, and then I would climb onto the bench and start to pound the keys. I think she decided to teach me because she couldn't take any more of my banging. I was a diligent student, but I didn't love to practice; I found it isolating. When I was ten, I told my mother I was quitting piano. She sat me down and explained I was too young to make that decision. So I kept on, and I've always been grateful for her advice. She taught me discipline.

I grew to love the piano, and music was my first major in college. When I was in graduate school at Stanford, I taught piano. It was easier than waiting tables. Then I realized the limits of my musical talent and decided to find another career.

After I finally left Washington and returned to Stanford in 2009, I regained my interest in playing. I still take lessons every week and occasionally play at charity events. In 2010, I played a benefit in Philadelphia with Aretha Franklin. Aretha called and asked me to do it. How could I refuse the Queen of Soul? In 2013, I did a concert with the Omaha Symphony, where I played the first movement of Schumann's piano concerto in A minor from memory, which I hadn't done since I was eighteen. The head of neurology at Stanford Medical School told me I'd done my neural plasticity a big favor.

At the other end of the spectrum, I'm an avid football fan. I was an only child, so my dad didn't have much choice, but his love of the game was infectious. Every August the Street and Smith pro- and college-football reports would come out and Dad and I would rush down to the corner drugstore to buy them. We would come home, sit together, and go through them page by page. It's one of my favorite memories.

All during my childhood, I was a competitive figure skater. I wasn't very good, but it was my sport. I believe the discipline of getting up every day and practicing, striving for perfection, is good training for anyone who wants to be successful. You can transfer that discipline into other pursuits.

I've always liked that sense of getting better at something. I play golf, and when fellow golfers tell me they play for fun, I always think: You have fun playing badly?

Of course, I've been on the receiving end of considerable criticism over the years. No one enjoys that, but if you're going to do anything of consequence, harsh opinions will come your way. Praise comes, too, but it's the criticism that you have to steel yourself for. You can't ignore it, because there's the possibility it contains some truth, and that you might learn something. But if you constantly doubt yourself, you don't get anything done.

Throughout it all, whenever I need strength and inspiration, all I have to do is look at the five leather-bound books sitting on my mantelpiece. That's when I am reminded that I was lifted on some very strong shoulders.

WILLARD SCOTT

Fans of NBC's Today Show *know that one of Willard Scott's most memorable moments came when he performed an impersonation of Carmen Miranda, the 1940s Brazilian samba singer, dancer, and actress, famous for wearing a bowl of fruit on her head. But what the fans may not know is why he did that. Turns out, fellow* Today Show *staffer Bryant Gumbel did a report on a museum being built in Rio de Janeiro to honor Miranda. Gumbel offered to make a donation to one of Willard's favorite charities if Willard would dress as Miranda and appear live on the show. He did. Memorably.*

Have you ever asked a question about someone and gotten the answer, "Oh, he's always been that way!" That is what I have said about Willard. Many people are defined by events, moments in time, or other people in their lives. For Willard, like some special people you may know, his greatest influence is simply the passion and joy he has for life.

I was born in Alexandria, Virginia, in 1934, at the height of the Great Depression. My father, Herman, was a North Carolina boy, raised on a farm. When he was a young man, working as a farmhand, the owner of the farm tried to stiff him for $25. He got mad and walked off the job, leaving the mule and plow right in the field. Then he got on a train, went to Danville, Virginia, and got a job at Dan River Mills, which produced textiles. He quickly realized he didn't like factory work any more than he did farming. So he applied for a job with Metropolitan Life in Alexandria and was hired to sell insurance door-to-door.

My dad was just a plain nice guy who had a great personality. My wackiness comes from him. He may not have dressed up like Carmen Miranda, but he always got a laugh out of people. He loved his clients, and they loved him. When I was a little kid, I'd tag along on his rounds to clients' houses to collect their weekly payment of a big fat quarter. One lady was just crazy about Dad, and we'd always arrive to find her house smelling of fresh-baked gingerbread. She'd say, "Oh, Herman, you must have a piece. And you, too, Willard."

At heart, my father was an optimist and a humanist. He cared about his family and his clients. We grew to be true friends, and he was the best man at my wedding.

My mother, Thelma, was a saint. I know that's a cliché, but in Mom's case it's true. Like Dad, she was from country stock. She was loving and caring and taught me to be kind and courteous to everyone I met. I think Mom knew my performing ability before I did. One day when I was about ten, I came home from school and she said, "Sonny, I read in the paper today they're going to do a play in town and they're looking for someone to play young George Washington. Why don't you try out?" I auditioned and got my first role.

When I was eight, Mom took me to the movies in Washington. Afterward, she wanted to do some shopping, which didn't interest me. So I wandered over to the nearby Earle Building, home of my favorite radio station, WTOP. I took the elevator up to the fifth floor, got off, introduced myself to the very nice receptionist, and told her I was a fan of the station. She took me on a little tour that ended in the control room. She told me, "You can sit here if you stay very quiet." She pointed through the plate glass to the recording studio. "That man will be broadcasting live."

The man she was pointing to was the soon-to-be legendary journalist Eric Sevareid. At the time, he was an international correspondent for CBS; he had just gotten back from Burma, where he had been lost in the jungle for several months. I sat there enthralled as Sevareid recounted every detail of his ordeal. I was also awed and fascinated by the studio itself—the microphones, the soundproofing, the hushed but charged atmosphere, the large control panel dotted with dials, all of it.

The next day I set to work building my own radio station in our finished basement. My parents bought me a little oscillator, an electronic device that enabled me to broadcast about 150 feet in every direction. Saturday was show day, and I enlisted my neighborhood friends to join me on the air. We would read the news, play tunes on a phonograph, and chatter away.

Jimmy Rudin, who is a rabbi today, was the Edward R. Murrow of our little group—he would crawl under the daybed so the sound would be muffled and present "Commentary with James Rudin." This wasn't a nonprofit enterprise—we sold commercials to the local shopping center for twenty-five cents a spot.

One Saturday morning about six months after we started, three men in leather jackets showed up at my house, looking none too happy. They were from the Federal Communications Commission, and they told us that our signal was reaching National Airport—and Pan Am's radios were picking up kids talking and playing records. So ended my basement radio station.

My station may have been shuttered by the FCC, but my passion for radio was undiminished. When I was sixteen I got hired as a page at WRC-AM, the NBC-owned radio station in Washington. I ran errands, greeted visitors, and generally did anything I was told.

One day former First Lady Eleanor Roosevelt came in to do *American Forum of the Air*, a popular talk show. As a page, it was my job to take her coat, which she handed me with a warm smile. I didn't want to hang it in the hall with all the other coats, so I took it to the vice president's office and hung it up there. About an hour later I was sent out to get some muffins for the crew. When I came back, Mrs. Roosevelt had left and the station manager grabbed me, asking,

"What the hell did you do with Eleanor Roosevelt's coat? She had to leave without it!" I awkwardly explained where I had stashed it. Mrs. Roosevelt had gone to the Washington Press Club, and I hustled over there with her coat. She couldn't have been more gracious, accepting the coat and my red face with a bemused, "Thank you, young man."

I juggled my page job with finishing high school, working weekends and school vacations. I was eager to try my hand at announcing, and I auditioned several times, but was never hired. Then one of the regular announcers left for vacation, the substitute was unavailable, and my boss said, "What the hell, let Scott do it. It's only for two weeks." I guess I did an adequate job because when the announcer returned, I became a regular substitute.

After college, WRC hired me as a regular performer on their new afternoon children's TV show called *Barn Party*. The show was hosted by Betsy Stelk, who held forth in a barn wearing an evening dress and wielding a little wand, sort of like the Good Witch in *The Wizard of Oz*. I was Farmer Willard and most of my cast mates were puppets. One of the puppeteers was a young fellow named Jim Henson, and our puppets were precursors of the Muppets, who made their first appearance a year later on another WRC kid's show.

I was quickly becoming a very busy guy. My bosses at WRC had heard a college show I did with friend Ed Walker (who recently passed away), and they gave us our own radio program, *The Joy Boys*, which debuted in 1955 and stayed on the air until 1974. The show was mostly improvisational comedy; we did a lot of satire, including a takeoff on the *Huntley-Brinkley Report* called *The Washer-Dryer Report*. We wrote all our own material and played a lot of different characters. Eddie was amazing with voices—he did Maxwell Smart, Richard Nixon, cartoon characters, you name it.

About a year after *The Joy Boys* debuted, I enlisted in the navy. After completing basic training, I was sent to Guantanamo Bay, Cuba, where I was stationed on a destroyer offshore. One day the regular weatherman on the base's radio station got laryngitis, and I filled it. That was my first time doing the weather.

Soon after I left the navy, I was back on television. *Barn Party* had earned me a name as a kid's performer, so when the station bought the local rights to *Bozo the Clown*, I was cast in the role.

It was a lot of fun being Bozo, especially in Washington, which is full of clowns who don't wear makeup. I went to the White House early in the Kennedy presidency; John-John was an infant and not around, but Bozo got to meet Caroline and the president.

In time, Bozo took his toll. I played him from 1959 to 1962, doing a one-hour live show every day as well as numerous public appearances. It was physically exhausting, especially coupled with my *Joy Boys* duties, and I almost had a nervous breakdown. Many of my appearances were at McDonald's restaurants, and when I left the Bozo show, I helped the company develop Ronald McDonald, its clown mascot. I was almost thirty and felt I was getting a little too old to be a clown.

I continued to cohost *The Joy Boys* and then, in 1970, I became the on-air weatherman for WRC. I loved the job because the weather report leaves room to be fun and spontaneous. Weather and I turned out to be a perfect storm.

One day Washington bureau chief Bill Small came into the studio and said, "Willard, how would you like to do the *Today Show* weather?" I went up to New York, and the first couple of months were a little rough. Then I began to get more mail than anyone else on the show. Of course, a lot of it was from viewers asking the network to take me off the air.

My saluting centenarians on their birthdays and married couples on their seventy-fifth wedding anniversary started as a fluke. I got a card from a fan that read, "My uncle is turning 100. Could you please mention him on TV?" Paul Harvey had done it on radio, and I always thought it was cute, so why not do it on television? I did it and never gave it a second thought. Then about a week later I got two cards, then four, and then six.

I've been lucky enough to meet some memorable ones. There was a gal named Reba Kelly in Minneapolis, who I met at a cocktail party. She looked like a classic hundred-year-old, with little wire glasses, wearing a blouse with a lace collar, her hair done up in a bun—except that she was drinking Jack Daniels and smoking a cigarette. I thought, "God, that's my kind of woman. I want to live to be a hundred years old and be just like Reba."

Entertaining folks is one hell of a way to make a living.

I was inspired at a young age by my mom, who taught me to be kind and decent, and by my dad, who taught me to laugh and see the bright side of life. Certainly, I was influenced by an inherent love for entertaining. After that, I just went along for the ride.

TOM SULLIVAN

Tom Sullivan lost his eyesight in infancy, but he acquired a keen sense of perception. He always suspected, for example, his father ended up with some of the money from the famous 1950 Boston Brink's robbery, in which $1.2 million was stolen and only $58,000 was ever recovered. This theory was bolstered when Tom went to college and his father showed up in the dean's office carrying two suitcases full of cash and proceeded to pay Tom's tuition. It was one of the many twists in his memorable journey.

It's impossible not to be inspired by Tom Sullivan. His perseverance and success, in the face of his disability, is exemplary. But there is more to Tom's defining moments than overcoming adversity. I was more moved by his keen perception of life than by his many accomplishments. Tom shows us that there is more than one way to "see" the world.

My story starts in 1947 in Boston, where I was born three months premature. I was put in an incubator into which too much oxygen was pumped. It caused irreparable damage to the blood vessels in my eyes, and from then on, I was blind.

Things were different back then. My parents took me to see a top-flight ophthalmologist. The man examined my eyes, then turned to my parents and said, "Mr. and Mrs. Sullivan, your child is blind. Institutionalize him." Then he walked out of the room.

I grew up in West Roxbury, an Irish Catholic neighborhood in Boston. My father, Thomas Sr., owned nine pubs, managed prizefighters, and was a bookie. Dad was a colorful character. He was born in the village of Kinsale on Ireland's west coast, and his family came to America when he was nine years old. Two weeks later, his father died. Dad dropped out of school and got a job. Over the ensuing years, he worked as everything from a delivery boy for the *Boston Globe* to a stevedore. He got lucky in 1920 when the Eighteenth Amendment to the Constitution (a.k.a. Prohibition) took effect. He immediately got a job running booze; at night, he would pilot small speedboats out to larger ships in Boston Harbor and ferry cases of whiskey back to shore. He made a small fortune as a bootlegger, and by the time I came along, he owned those nine Irish pubs.

Dad was into Boston politics. One of his good friends was Congressman Tip O'Neill, who later became Speaker of the House. He also "lent a hand" when John F. Kennedy ran for the House and Senate and again when he ran for president in 1960.

I think the secret to Dad's success was our back porch. He was a networker before the word existed. On Sundays, every Irish politician and police captain in the city would drop by after mass. A lot of them were still half in the bag from the night before.

Even with the hangovers, deals were made on our back porch. I know this firsthand, because I would listen, fascinated by the rhythm and cadences of the speech as much as by the content of what was being said. My mother would bring out platters of bacon and eggs. She had one rule: every time you swore, you had to tack a dollar up on the wall. I think I went to college on the singles that lined that wall, or at least they supplemented the alleged Brink's job loot.

Like a lot of heavy drinkers, my dad had a dark, violent side, but he handled my blindness matter-of-factly. He wanted a rough-and-tumble son who played in the street with the others kids. What he got was a son who had to be fenced in the backyard.

My mother wanted me to concentrate on my studies, on music and art, on my mind. My parents had a lot of arguments about me and they divorced when I was twelve. I took it hard.

I was sent to the Perkins School for the Blind outside Boston. I hated it. I acted out in many ways and was expelled from school several times. On this one occasion, I was sent to the principal's office for stealing food from the kitchen, a rather minor offense at the time, and told to sit in the punishment chair for the rest of the morning. As I was sitting there, Helen Keller walked in. She was an alumnae of the school and was visiting on what I believe was her eightieth birthday. She had a companion, who held Keller's palm and spelled out words in it. Her companion told her that I was in trouble.

"Why?" Miss Keller asked.

"Because he acts out."

A moment later I sensed her approaching me. She took my hand and spelled out, "Little boy, they tell me you're a devil. Is that right?"

I spelled out, "Yes."

She spelled out, "Good, keep it up!"

I took that as a badge of honor.

Despite my behavior, I did rather well at Perkins, especially in athletics (wrestling and track) and music. There was one music teacher I liked, an African American man named Hank Santos. Hank was a brilliant pianist who took an interest in me. It was in his classes that my love for music took hold.

During one lesson, I told him I was sick of playing Bach and Chopin.

"What do you want to play?" he asked.

"I want to play standards, and I want to sing, too."

Hank gave me braille sheet music for the Great American Songbook and assigned me songs made famous by the likes of Ella Fitzgerald and Billie Holiday. One day he asked if I would come to his house and play for some friends of his.

I agreed, and the following Saturday afternoon, my mother drove me to Hank's house. I met his wife, Nancy, whose voice was warm and welcoming. Then I sat at the piano and played for about twenty people. When I was finished there was applause, which I instantly loved.

One man approached me and said, "So, young man, Hank tells me you're a pretty angry kid. Why is that?"

I started my litany: I'd been cheated by blindness, the world wasn't giving me a chance, I didn't belong, I couldn't find a way to be equal to sighted people.

I could sense he was listening. *Really* listening. When I was done, he said, "You've got a lot of stuff you're complaining about. But is it really getting you anywhere? You can't see, but you're clearly blessed in other ways."

There was something about the man's voice that just reached down into my heart and opened it up. You hear those things when you are blind. Of course, I was still an angry teenager, so the best response I could muster was, "Yeah. Okay. Thanks."

"Hank and I were roommates at Boston University, and I'm going to ask him to keep me posted on you," the man added as he walked away. Later my teacher told me his name was Martin Luther King, a name I didn't recognize at the time.

I finally graduated Perkins and, believe it or not, went on to Providence College and Harvard, where President Nathan Pusey told people I was the smartest blind guy he'd ever met. That seemed like a dumb thing to say. Wasn't I just plain smart?

I felt most at home when I was sitting at a piano, playing and singing; I also noticed that it charmed the ladies. Music became my ticket. When I was a junior, I started playing in local bars, and that summer I found a job performing at a restaurant called Deacon's Perch in Yarmouth on Cape Cod.

I attracted some regulars—one couple came in every night, ordered drinks, and asked me to play their favorites. They were lovely, upbeat people and, after a few visits, introduced themselves as Betty White and Allen Ludden. They were playing summer stock on the Cape and liked to come in after the show to unwind.

It's no exaggeration to say that Betty White changed my life.

One night, a woman asked me to play "By the Time I Get to Phoenix." The song brought her to tears and when I was finished, she said, "Do you mind if I ask you a question?"

"Go ahead."

"How did you go blind?"

"I don't want to talk about it."

She pressed me.

"I was a pilot, got shot down, and spent years in a prison camp, and you're the first woman I've met since I got out."

Betty White heard this, laughed, and turned to the woman who had asked me the question. "Young lady," she said, "this kid is full of shit." After the woman had retreated, Betty said to me, "Forget her. But there's a lovely girl, and she's been coming in every night to hear you. You should see the look in her eyes. Come with me." So Betty took my hand and marched me across the room to the young woman's table and made the introductions. The upshot? Patty and I have been married for forty-six years.

After that summer on Cape Cod, Betty and Allen arranged for me to appear on *The Mike Douglas Show* in New York, and then they invited me out to California, where I did *The Tonight Show* with Johnny Carson, which jump-started my career as a singer, composer, and actor. I was a headliner in Vegas, appeared in numerous television shows, including a recurring role in *Highway to Heaven* with Michael Landon, and sang the "Star Spangled Banner" at Super Bowl X. I wrote a book entitled *If You Could See What I Hear* that did well and was made into a movie.

I was booked on *Good Morning America* to talk about my book. Charlie Gibson did the interview and afterward the *GMA* producer asked me how I thought it went.

"I thought it sucked," I said.

"Why?"

"Gibson didn't have any insight into who I am as a person, and he hadn't done his homework. I think I could do a better job."

"You do?"

"Yes, a blind person knows how to listen."

"Alright," he said. "I'll give you a camera crew. Go out and shoot three stories. If I run them, I'll give you a chance to do more."

That's how I got hired at *Good Morning America*. At first, I did upbeat stories about people who were beating the odds. Then their celebrity correspondent quit, and I was given her beat. The movie *10* had just come out, and my first assignment was to interview Bo Derek. Some at the network laughed at the idea of sending a blind guy to interview a woman considered one of the most beautiful in the world, but I went anyway.

I thought a lot about what to ask Bo, and my first question was, "People tell me you are a perfect physical ten, but I can't see you, so how do I know you are beautiful?" She didn't answer for a second and then she said, "I'm beautiful inside as well as out. But nobody is interested in the fact that I can think or that I'm studying to get a master's in literature or that I'm committed to the environment or that I love animals or that I could love a husband who's thirty years older. All they know is that I have a good ass in a bathing suit."

Much of my life, I have felt the same way. Not about the ass in a bathing suit, but about the way people respond to meeting me, a blind guy. But I'll say this: we all have some disabilities and we just have to get over them. Yes, I am blind, but I play golf (Jack Nicklaus once told me, "The best thing I can say about your swing is that you can't see it"), ski, run marathons, and have even jumped out of airplanes. In my quest to excel and have a normal life, I have even driven a car. Scary, huh?

I didn't pay much attention to him at the time, but Martin Luther King Jr. was right when he said I was "blessed in other ways." We all are, no matter what obstacles we think have been placed in our way. We just have to stop complaining about what is wrong and bad in life and start looking for what is right and good. Martin Luther King Jr. inspired me with his wisdom, and Helen Keller inspired me with her attitude. When she learned I was "acting out" and advised me to "keep it up," she was telling me to use that edge I had in life as a tool. We all need something to drive us and keep us focused in life, and there is nothing better to do that than a little bit of an attitude.

PETER UEBERROTH

At the 1972 Summer Olympics in Munich, a Palestinian terrorist group called Black September killed nine Israeli athletes. The 1976 Montreal Olympics cost $5 billion, a debt that would not be paid off until 2005. Because of Russia's invasion of Afghanistan in December 1979, the United States and more than sixty other countries boycotted the 1980 Olympics in Moscow. Given this recent history of the games, the announcement of the 1984 Olympics in Los Angeles, with Russia's planned boycott, was greeted with much skepticism. And yet a relatively unknown businessman, Peter Ueberroth, successfully ran the games, ended them with a $240 million profit, and was named Time *magazine's Man of the Year.*

We think of a turning point as a person, an event, or a moment in time that changes us. Sometimes it's not a single instance but a series of decisions influenced by a defining principle that we are taught early in life.

It was 1959. My wife, Ginny, and I were enjoying an anniversary lunch on Waikiki Beach in Honolulu, where we were living at the time. That sounds glamorous until I explain that it was a monthly anniversary, and that we were ordering from the less expensive right side of the menu. Like most newlyweds, we didn't have much money, so we decided to celebrate our anniversary monthly instead of yearly because it added a celebratory note to our hardworking lives. We were sitting on this lovely lanai enjoying ice teas and waiting for our food, when a well-dressed African American couple entered the restaurant. It was late in the afternoon, and there were plenty of empty tables, but the couple was seated at the worst table in the place, right by the swinging doors going into the kitchen. They knew they had been slighted, even discriminated against, but they handled it with grace.

"That's not right," Ginny said. "We ought to do something." I debated talking to the manager, who I knew because I worked across the street, but Ginny cut me off by saying, "Why not invite them to come sit with us?"

"Good idea." I walked over to their table and said, "My wife and I would be delighted if you would join us for lunch."

"That's a kind offer," the man said, "We accept."

So they sat with us, and we had a lovely lunch. They were as nice as could be, and we all laughed and had a good time. I didn't want to pester them with a lot of questions. He did mention he was in town to give a speech, but, the truth is, I didn't pay much attention. We split the check and shook hands good-bye. Ginny went home to get ready for her evening job at Sears, and I went back to work at Great Lakes Airlines.

Several days later, I saw a picture of our lunch-mate in the Honolulu newspaper: he was Reverend Martin Luther King Jr.

The civil rights movement was still in its early stages at that point, but I was a supporter. I'd been on the football, baseball, and swim teams in high school. I knew that being a team player had nothing to do with skin color. It's about hard work, focus, and cooperation.

After that lunch, I paid closer attention to the civil rights movement. The more engaged I became, the more passionate my support and admiration became. Here were our fellow Americans demanding their basic civil rights, and doing it with extraordinary resolve, dignity, discipline, and a deep and oft-stated commitment to nonviolence, despite the terrible violence perpetrated against them. Their cause was just and their means exemplary.

If it hadn't been for my father, Victor Ueberroth, I may never have had that life-changing lunch. He took the words "all men are created equal" very seriously, and he let my siblings and me know that we were expected to treat everyone we met with respect. He dropped out of school after the ninth grade. It was during the Depression, his family had little money, and he was eager to find a job. But he was a voracious reader and a self-educated man. We had encyclopedias in the house and he was always the first to look up subjects that came up during dinner-table discussions.

Dad sold aluminum roofs and siding mainly to farmers, and he was away from home Monday through Friday, so those nights when he was home were precious to us. Dinner with Dad was never boring; he was curious about the world, and we touched on every topic. He loved maps and discussing global politics, telling us, "We're all citizens of the world."

Our family didn't have the money to travel the world, but we saw a lot of the United States because Dad was transferred a fair amount. Once a territory was sold through, we were moved to another one. I went to school in Illinois, Wisconsin, Pennsylvania, California (northern and southern), Iowa, and Nebraska. I went to college on a water polo scholarship at San Jose State and after graduation got a job with Great Lakes Airlines in Honolulu. It was a tiny airline, and I did everything except fly the plane: I took reservations, checked in passengers, and loaded baggage.

That experience inspired me to found my own travel company, First Travel, which eventually grew into the second-largest travel business in the country.

In 1979, a private committee of Los Angeles citizens and Mayor Tom Bradley (the first African American mayor of a major city) asked me to serve as president of the 1984 Olympic Games in Los Angeles. The lessons I'd learned in business, from my father, and from the civil rights movement, all guided me. When I found myself in stressful situations, I would think of Dr. King's equanimity in the face of far more serious challenges. Later that year, I became the commissioner of Major League Baseball. I held the job for five years, during which time the league broke attendance records each season; we also instituted policy guidelines that significantly improved minority hiring throughout MLB, not just on the field.

In 1986, I was touched to be named one of two grand marshals of the Atlanta parade in honor of Dr. King's birthday being made a national holiday. I was especially humbled because the other grand marshal was Rosa Parks.

The parade was on January 20, 1986, and it was really cold in Atlanta that morning. An estimated one million African Americans lined the parade route.

I met Rosa before the parade started, and she was delightful, modest, and charming, with a beguiling smile, but you could sense her quiet strength. There were two white Cadillac convertibles, and we each got in one as we waited for the parade to start. I hadn't packed for the weather and was freezing. Rosa came over and said, "You look cold."

"I didn't get the memo about the weather."

We laughed and she said, "I have an idea. We don't need two cars, why don't you ride with me? I've got a big pile of blankets."

"That's the best offer I've had all day."

And so for the next two and a half hours, as we made our way slowly along the parade route, I acted as child- and baby-relay as one parent after another handed me their child, which I dutifully presented to Rosa to be kissed or touched, after which I handed the child back. It was just about the best job I ever had, and one of the most moving days of my life. Lots of pictures were taken, and I imagine there are kids today who look at family photo albums and ask, "Who's that white guy with Rosa Parks?"

In 1992, after having left baseball, I led the Rebuild Los Angeles project, again at the request of Mayor Bradley, which sought to rebuild and heal the city after the riots that followed the acquittal of the police officers who had been videotaped beating Rodney King.

Once again, my mission was guided by my father's belief in equality and the lessons of cooperation, respect, and unity I'd learned from the civil rights movement.

When I look back at that Waikiki lunch over a half century ago, I first realize how much credit goes to Ginny. She was the one who invited that young African American couple to join us for lunch and put in to action what my father had taught me at a young age about equality. I was just twenty-two years old, but, thanks to my nineteen-year-old bride, I met a man whose courage, decency, and faith not only changed America and the world, but also changed the life of one very lucky fellow.

Sometimes, we can credit what inspires and changes us in life to a parent or a spouse, the people we meet, or the jobs we are given to do. More often than not, it adds up to be a little bit of all of them.

JUDY WOODRUFF

Journalist Judy Woodruff tells the story of the time she had just finished giving her two-month-old son Jeffrey a bottle in the White House press office, when she and her husband, columnist Al Hunt, were summoned to meet with President Reagan. With no time to give the baby an over-the-shoulder pat, they were escorted into the Oval Office, where a smiling President Reagan scooped Jeffrey up and started telling stories about his own children. He finished by singing a nursery rhyme about riding a horse: "This is the way the ladies ride . . ." bouncing the baby up and down, first gently, and then more vigorously as he moved to "the way the gentlemen ride," and finally "the way the cowboys ride!" Through it all, Judy and Al were holding their breath, envisioning Jeffrey spoiling the president's jacket just before his next scheduled appointment—a meeting with the head of an African state. But Jeffrey came through it all, calm and collected, mesmerized as so many were by the Reagan charm.

We all experience love. In many ways, whom we love, when we love, and who loves us, changes us. But sometimes love, unconditional family love, is so powerful in our lives that it becomes our greatest influence.

I don't want my story to be depressing. It's about one of life's unexpected turns—the loss of many of my son's abilities—but it has also been a source of profound inspiration, and happiness.

When Al and I started talking about getting married, one of the points we agreed on from the start was that we wanted children. Both of us love kids. And I think, in the absence of career demands, I would have had more children than our three. In our business, we're on call seven days a week. And that suits us, because, to be honest, Al and I are both driven people. We thrive on being busy, and we both love journalism. And because we also loved our family, we felt incredibly fortunate. We couldn't get enough of the life we were living.

And then something happened that shattered us. It's always there, always hard to think about, and even harder to talk about. But in the end, it's a story of hope.

Our first child, Jeffrey, had a mild type of spina bifida, which is a birth defect that involves the spinal cord. When he was ten months old, Jeffrey had a shunt implanted. It's a tube that drains excess fluid from the cerebrospinal cavity in the head. This is a routine treatment; some babies with spina bifida have one put in at birth. Of course, I was terribly worried, but Jeffrey never had a problem. As he grew up, he could do so many things that most children with spina bifida can't. He learned to walk on schedule, at thirteen months. He learned to ride a bike. He was an active kid. He played soccer. He managed the high school wrestling and football teams. He loved to ski. He was always an achiever academically.

Then, in 1998, when Jeffrey was in tenth grade, his doctor told us that his shunt was failing and needed to be replaced. We were surprised, and Jeffrey was unhappy that his summer plans might be interrupted—he was interested in medicine and had been accepted as a summer intern at the Food and Drug Administration. So we scheduled the procedure for right after his final exams. He was supposed to be in the hospital for a day or two, recuperate at home for another couple of days, and then he could be off to his internship.

Instead, two weeks later, there was a complication that landed Jeff back in the hospital. Doctors proposed a different procedure to solve the problem, but something went terribly wrong. Jeffrey suffered a serious brain injury during this surgery. He didn't wake up when it was over. At first, we didn't know if he would live. He remained in a coma for more than two months. For another three months after that, he couldn't eat or speak.

Al and I and our two other children, Lauren, nine, and Benjamin, eleven, were in a state of shock. It was impossible to process what had happened, and yet we had to keep functioning.

We had Jeffrey transferred to the Kennedy Krieger Institute, a pediatric neuro-rehabilitation hospital adjacent to Johns Hopkins in Baltimore, Maryland. The medical and therapeutic teams there are among the best in the world. They worked with us to give Jeff the best possible support as he emerged from the coma and had to relearn how to swallow and speak, and get physical and vocational therapy. We, meanwhile, moved to Baltimore and commuted to our jobs in Washington for five months. I took a leave of absence from CNN.

Once we knew he would survive, the questions were when could he come home and how much better would he get? And the hard truth was that Jeffrey's doctors were not optimistic. They told us he would on some level be functional again, but that he would never fully recover.

We willed ourselves to go on. We became close to several of Jeffrey's doctors. One of them took us to dinner and gave us advice that I know helped us find a way to cope. He told us that this was the kind of life-altering event that all too often ends a marriage. He told us there was going to be a permanent strain on us as a couple, that we would need to find a way to support not just Jeffrey and our other children, but also each other. And this became something we were acutely conscious of, and still are now, some fifteen years later. We kept our eyes open to the challenge of staying together through it all. The fact that we truly love each other has made a huge difference.

When Jeffrey finally got home he was at the functional level of a third grader. He could no longer walk and was using a wheelchair.

He didn't have the use of his right arm. One eye was permanently closed, and his vision in the other eye was impaired. His short-term memory was gone. And his speech was severely compromised—he could barely make himself understood. I couldn't imagine what kind of life he was going to have.

And then something quite wonderful happened. A group of Jeffrey's former teachers volunteered to tutor him. And his friends became regular visitors. Someone told us about using recent college graduates who were bound for medical school as yearlong companions. So we did that. It was great for Jeffrey and great for the students, who have told us they are better doctors today for having had that experience.

Today, Jeffrey has a pretty good life. All the generous people who helped him contributed to that. But it is mostly because of Jeffrey's courage and determination. He missed a year of school, but then went back to the eleventh grade, where, thanks to his teachers, he mostly caught up with what he had missed. After high school, he attended a local community college. That was challenging because, although the school had some accommodations for students with disabilities, it didn't have any with Jeffrey's complicated needs. His challenges are unique.

Jeffrey is as smart as he was before he was injured. But because of his physical disabilities, and especially because of his impaired short-term memory, every day for him is like climbing Mount Everest. It takes him much longer to do everything. The memory issue makes school difficult. He remembers most all events in the past—he can recall where we went on vacation when he was ten or an important conversation from a week ago. But, until he's prompted, he usually can't remember what movie he saw last night or who called him a few minutes ago. So to learn something, to memorize information, Jeffrey has to go over it again and again and again, until it somehow becomes part of the memory he can access, so he's able to take a test. It is a lot of work.

When his younger brother, Benjamin, was nearing the end of high school and talking about going away to college, Jeffrey told us he wanted to do the same. Al and I wondered how we could make that happen. We looked all over the country for a school that could take a student like Jeffrey. In the end we found St. Andrews Presbyterian College in North Carolina. At that time, in 2005, they not only accepted students with significant physical disabilities, they had a special dormitory for them. When we visited the school, it was an eye-opening—and mind-opening—experience. There were students tooling around campus in wheelchairs, going to class, hanging out with their friends—leading a life as close to normal as possible. That's where Jeffrey went and where he earned his degree in 2010.

Just before he graduated, Jeffrey surprised us again. He said he didn't want to live at home with his parents after he was done with school. By now we had a network of friends and experts in the disability community, so we started looking for a place where he could live on his own. We eventually found Target Community and Educational Services, in Westminster, Maryland. It was founded a couple of decades ago with a gift from an aerospace executive who had a grown daughter with disabilities.

Jeffrey graduated, and after a short visit home, he moved to Westminster. He lives in a group home and works at McDaniel College. Al and I feel terrifically fortunate to have found the right situation for him. And he is happy there. He comes home about once a month, we take vacations together, and we have a great time. But he's always eager to get back to Westminster.

Before this happened, I thought I had my life and family pretty well figured out. What happened with Jeffrey taught me not only that profound change can happen in an instant, but also that you can find inspiration where you least expect it. I would never wish our experience on anyone, and yet seeing what our son has accomplished against such long odds has been unimaginably rewarding. When you meet Jeffrey Hunt and see what it takes for him to get through the day—and how he does it with a positive outlook and a sense of humor—it makes your own problems seem very small. Jeffrey knows the details of what happened to him. And he knows he could spend the rest of his life embittered. Al and I could spend the rest of our lives being angry. But we take our cue from Jeffrey. We get on with life. That's what Jeffrey has inspired us to do.

LEE WOODRUFF

In December 2005, Bob Woodruff replaced our good friend Peter Jennings, who died that year from complications from lung cancer, as anchor of ABC World News Tonight. *Almost exactly one year later, Bob traveled to Iraq to meet with American troops prior to President Bush's State of the Union address. There, he and his cameraman were critically wounded by a roadside bomb.*

Lee's turning point in life is of course inspiring, but it's in her telling here that the true defining moment comes through. Sometimes in life our only choice is to keep moving forward, one single step at a time, no matter how difficult the path or how long it takes.

The call that changed my life came at 7:00 a.m. on January 9, 2006. I was asleep in a Disney World hotel when the phone rang. I was sure it was my wake-up call—the kids and I were planning a big day exploring the park—but it wasn't the front desk. It was David Westin, the head of ABC News, telling me that my husband, Bob Woodruff, coanchor of the *ABC World News Tonight*, had been seriously injured in Iraq.

I heard the words "improvised explosive device," "head wound," and "shrapnel," but they didn't fully register. I hung up and without consciously thinking about it I pushed all my shock, anxiety, and grief aside for the sake of our four children. In addition to breaking the news to them, I had to call Bob's parents and my parents and then get on a flight home to Westchester, New York.

I went outside and walked around a little lake on the hotel grounds. As I circled it, I dialed both sets of parents. I also called David back and told him he could release the news. Then I took a deep breath and went back into the hotel to give my children the news, that their father had been injured by a bomb.

People often ask me how I got through it all, where did I find the strength. But the truth is when you are a parent, you don't have the luxury of collapsing, as attractive as the thought of a couple of Valium and a bottle of Jack Daniels might have been at the time.

The kids, who were sharing a suite, were unfortunately already awake. Mack, who was fifteen, was watching CNN and knew something was wrong. He was being grown-up, stoic, his face filled with concern. Seeing the news on television hit me like a punch. I could feel tears coming. I went into the bathroom, but before I had a chance to cry, Cathryn, who was twelve years old, opened the door. She looked vulnerable. "Daddy's going to be okay," I said. I knew I had to believe those words. For the kids, for me, and for Bob.

The twins, Nora and Claire, were five and they thought Daddy's injury was like a hurt they would experience. Mack and Cathryn were scared but they stayed calm. I told them that their father was in the hospital and was being taken care of by great military doctors. I kept it simple. For their sakes—and mine. ABC/Disney made a plane available to take us home and send me on to the hospital in Germany where Bob was being transported. There were a lot of decisions to make and, in a way, that's what saved me.

I spoke to David several times that day and got more details. Bob and his cameraman, Doug Vogt, had been embedded with a US Army infantry unit near Taji, Iraq. It was supposed to be a mission to show how the Iraqis were stepping up their patrols and making the country safer. Bob and Doug were riding in a tank, rolling down a road that had been swept for bombs five minutes earlier. There was a stand of trees ahead by the road, and it was later presumed that immediately after the sweep an insurgent had run out, dug a hole, planted an IED, and covered it with rocks and dirt.

Bob and Doug were standing in the tank with their heads above the hatch. They were coming up to the trees when the insurgent triggered the bomb, most likely with a remote-controlled device. My husband and his cameraman were about twenty-five feet away when the bomb went off. Both Bob and Doug were hit by shrapnel, much of it rocks and dirt. A lot of that was embedded in Bob's face, skull, and back. His first words after the explosion were, "Am I alive?"

The goal of the bomb was to draw as many of our soldiers as possible out of their vehicles and then to pick them off with rifle fire. A fierce gunfight ensued. The medical helicopter that had been dispatched when the bomb went off received orders to turn around—it wasn't safe to land. There were two young medics onboard. According to their commander, one looked at the radio and said, "I didn't hear anything, did you?" The other answered, "I didn't hear a thing."

They landed the helicopter, loaded Bob and Doug, and flew them to Baghdad, where Bob's condition was assessed as critical. The doctors didn't expect him to live. They put him in another helicopter and flew him to the US Air Force hospital in Balad, Iraq, where they sawed off part of his skull to relieve pressure as his brain swelled. All of this took place within an hour.

After the surgery, Bob was airlifted to the army's Landstuhl Regional Medical Center in Germany.

Once inside the hospital, I was led to the ICU. I didn't know what to expect. The room was frigid; cold helps reduce swelling. Bob was behind a curtain. I pushed it back. He was lying on his back, on a ventilator with about eight tubes coming out of his body. Because I was on his right side and couldn't see the full extent of his head wound, I thought he looked pretty good. Then I walked to the other side of the bed. It was horrific: the left side of his face had been blasted with rocks and tattooed with dirt, sixteen centimeters of his skull had been removed, and his brain was bulging out, swollen to the size of a rugby ball. I was stunned. Then I thought, "Okay, he's in a superb hospital. The best doctors in the world are fixing him." One of the doctors offered to show me Bob's CAT scan and MRI. I declined. I wanted to stay in my little bubble of hope.

That day, I took charge, deciding who would see him. I wouldn't let in anyone who I felt might rush to judgment regarding his recovery. No naysayers. I heard years later someone said of me, "You've got to look out for the wife, nobody gets by her." I took that as a compliment. If everyone was expecting some kind of dumb blonde, they were mistaken. I was a mother lioness.

The next day, January 31, Bob was flown to Andrews Air Force Base outside Washington and transferred to Bethesda Naval Hospital in Bethesda, Maryland. Bob was in a coma for thirty-six days. Two and a half weeks after the injury, surgeons went into his neck to remove a marble-sized rock that had gone through most of his neck and come to rest one-tenth of a millimeter shy of his carotid artery.

Soon after the neck surgery, Bob got sepsis and pneumonia and came close to death a second time. Our children were asking a lot of questions. It was time for them to see him. I took Cathryn in first. We were holding hands, and as I reached for the curtain surrounding his bed, she squeezed my hand like a vise. When she saw her father, she cried, "I love you, Daddy!" and began to kiss him, on his forehead, his cheek, his hand. Bob started to cry. That was the first sign we had that he could hear us, that Bob was still in there, was still with us. "Maybe this might be okay," I thought.

The days passed slowly. I settled into an unsettled routine. It came down to fundamentals, which for me are the four Fs: family, friends, faith, and funny. Family and friends, of course, are crucial on a journey like this. You can't make it alone. Faith is another lynchpin. I've known people with all different levels of faith, and I've come to the conclusion that those who believe that there's something bigger than just us out there—whether they be Buddhist, Christian, Muslim, or whatever—tend to have a brighter outlook and recovery. And never underestimate the power of humor. When you joke and laugh, you weaken the power of the bad, at least temporarily.

After Bob's injury I began to investigate brain trauma. Then, retreating into my bubble of hope, I put my education on hold. I didn't want to go on Google or WebMD and scare myself silly, and I didn't want to ask the doctors a lot of detailed questions and hear worst-case scenarios. Of course, I picked up scraps of information in the hospital, but I wasn't actively seeking it. Then I was told that Bob could end up in a permanent vegetative state and that I should start looking at acute-care nursing homes. That was the day that I said to his doctor, "I want to know everything." I became a voracious student, reading whatever I could find, asking every question. And surprisingly, the knowledge gave me even more hope.

Then one morning I arrived at the hospital and noticed that the nurses were looking at me funny. I walked into Bob's room, and he was sitting up, his blue eyes bright, a smile on his face. He said, "Hey sweetie, where have you been?" As if I'd gone to Starbucks and taken too long. I kissed him and held his hand to my cheek, but part of me wanted to hit him on the good side of his head and say, "Let me tell you where I've been, mister." A medic was in the room, and she said, "He woke up at about 4:00 a.m. and he's been saying, 'Where is my life, where is my life?'" He was trying to say "wife." He got some points for that.

Just about every doctor in the hospital came to see Bob that day because that kind of spontaneous awakening is rare with a brain injury. It's usually a more gradual process. Almost the first question Bob asked was about the rest of the team. When he learned that Doug's injuries were less severe than his own, he relaxed.

We entered a new phase of his recovery. As expected, Bob's synapses sometimes fired in peculiar ways. He would make up words or insert the wrong word occasionally, and quite unexpectedly, use a French or Mandarin word. He'd learned French as a child and Mandarin as an adult. When you learn a second language before the age of six, it gets housed in one of the brain's filing cabinets. When you learn a language as an adult, it goes into a different filing cabinet. When he first woke up, his brain was reaching for the English file and not finding the right words, so it moved into the French file and then the Mandarin file.

After six weeks at Bethesda, Bob moved to a rehabilitation facility near our home. Although his progress was remarkable, it was erratic at times. His brain was reorganizing itself and connecting the neurons. When Bob cracked a stupid joke during a rehab session, the doctors asked me if it sounded like his sense of humor. I told them that stupid jokes had always been a specialty of his. They were watching to see if his personality had altered. That's really the hallmark of brain injuries—an introvert becomes an extrovert, or there is a lack of emotion or affect. It's another miracle that Bob escaped those outcomes—even if it does mean having to put up with stupid jokes.

After three weeks in inpatient rehab, Bob came home. Although he was walking, talking, laughing, and eager to get back to work, he was still fragile and hadn't yet had the piece of his skull replaced. The big unknown was the extent of the long-term damage to his cognitive abilities. One night not long after he came home, we went to the movies and saw *The Da Vinci Code*. As we walked out, Bob said, "I didn't understand any of that." My heart sank momentarily, but then I realized that I hadn't understood any of it either. It was a complicated plot and if I hadn't read the book, I would have missed much of it too.

When he first got home, Bob was joyous and buoyant. Once the initial euphoria faded, he began to understand the enormity of what he had lost and became depressed, but he didn't stay down for long. I can't say enough about his attitude. His positivity drove his recovery. He read, exercised, and asked the speech therapist to come in on weekends.

I had my down days. Sometimes I felt like a lifeguard who gets the drowning man to shore and then falls apart. And I did. Not in a public way, or in any way the kids saw, but what had been up came crashing down. I was a mess, completely depleted both emotionally and physically.

I learned to shrink my world down into bite-sized moments. If I couldn't get through a day at a time, I would get through an hour at a time. Every small achievement or milestone was a cause for celebration: Bob getting out of the hospital, regaining function, coming home, easing back into work. But the achievements came at a cost. I felt as if I was carrying an egg on a spoon through all of it.

I was holding it all together so much that there were times I wasn't present fully. One day I drove our children to school in my pajamas, and on the way, I rolled through a stop sign. I remember thinking, "Lee, you just aren't present. You should not be driving a car right now." I didn't want anything to happen to my children. I tried not to focus on how random life was.

One morning, I had gotten Bob off to rehab and the kids out the door to school. I walked into the living room and lay down on the couch. Suddenly I started sobbing. I'm not sure how long it went on before a voice in my head said, "It's going to be okay." I stopped crying and felt a sense of peace. Maybe I conjured up that voice to snap myself out of the crying jag, maybe I was just cried-out, or maybe it was part of my faith equation kicking in, a power bigger than me. Some years earlier a friend of mine who had terminal ovarian cancer said to me, "When bad things happen, you really have two choices— you can get bitter or you can get better. And nobody wants to be a bitter old lady." I have thought a lot about her words.

I knew that Bob's recovery was going to take time, and I didn't want anyone to count him out prematurely. So for almost a year, we lived a very private life. Once again, I was the fiercely protective gatekeeper. I needed Bob to feel confident before he faced the world. The better Bob got, the better I got.

A lot of people have told me it's a marvel that I came through the way I did. A New York psychiatrist friend took me out to talk to me. She told me she was fascinated by how "normal" I seemed after all the trauma. I didn't know if I should be insulted or flattered. I think the human spirit is more resilient than we give it credit for. I think my maternal instincts, my mother's heart, beside my love for Bob, drove a great deal of my behavior. I didn't want our children to be scarred by what had happened to our family, I wanted them to be strengthened by it. I wanted to expand their capacity to hope.

BOB WOODWARD

Deep Throat, one of the great political and journalistic mysteries of the twentieth century, was a secret source for Bob Woodward and Carl Bernstein's investigation into the misdeeds of President Richard Nixon and his administration, better known as Watergate. His identity was so secret that it was known only to Woodward, Bernstein, and Washington Post *editor Ben Bradlee. On May 31, 2005, thirty years after Richard Nixon resigned the presidency,* Vanity Fair *magazine revealed and Bob Woodward confirmed that the identity of Deep Throat was Mark Felt, the associate director of the FBI. Everyone always asks Bob about Deep Throat. But there is much more to his story.*

Like others in this book, Bob's defining moments clearly contribute to what he has accomplished in life as one of the greatest investigative journalists of all time. His turning points show us what we can discover about ourselves, and the world around us, if we open our eyes and take the time to observe, explore, and ask serious questions.

grew up in Wheaton, Illinois, during the 1950s. Wheaton, which is twenty-five miles west of Chicago, is the home of Wheaton College, where the evangelist Billy Graham went to school. The town had a pronounced moralistic culture where everyone lived the gospel Graham preached, at least on the surface.

My father was a lawyer. During high school, I had a part-time job working as a janitor at his small firm. I would spend an hour cleaning the office every weeknight, and on Saturday I would do a three- to four-hour shift. In the course of cleaning, I often saw files on the lawyers' desks. They piqued my curiosity, and I couldn't help but read some of them. I remember one file labeled with the names of a classmate's parents. It detailed a pretty grim divorce case.

The files pertaining to disposed cases were kept in the attic. One Saturday, I went up there and started looking through them. I read about tax fraud, infidelity, civil lawsuits, and criminal investigations—all pertaining to Wheaton residents, many of whom I knew. I quickly realized our apple pie town was something of a façade. For a boy of fifteen, who'd had a sheltered childhood, this was a revelation.

Those hours in the attic were my first exposure to the dichotomy between what people say and what they do. The disposed files became a powerful symbol for me. To this day, I listen to what people say and try to give them the benefit of the doubt, but at the same time, I always wonder whether there may be a more authentic version, a darker side of people and their behavior.

One of the disposed files contained the transcript of a tape recording made by a teenage girl who had worn a wire while she was having an affair with an official in the Wheaton school system. I remember being struck for the first time by the evidentiary purity of a tape recording. It's not someone's recollection, not a laundered, rescored version of what happened. It's the truth.

I went to Yale, where my study of history continued to provide me with examples of this disconnect between public utterance and truth. I learned this dissembling was most glaring when it came to politicians and others in positions of power. History doesn't come with all the cards turned face up. Much is hidden; you have to dig for it. While people's intentions may be good, their actions—usually for reasons of self-preservation—sometimes don't match their intentions. In his acceptance speech for the 1949 Nobel Prize for literature,

William Faulkner said, "The human heart in conflict with itself is the only thing worth writing about." His words planted a seed with me.

After Yale, I went into the navy. During my last year, I worked in communications at the Pentagon. As part of my job, I was exposed to some of the top-secret messages about the Vietnam War. While publicly the admirals, generals, and secretary of defense were delivering positive news, the information in those messages was often terribly negative. I remember one file reporting that a hotel in Hanoi had been bombed by mistake. Another revealed that the air strikes were not as effective as the military was claiming. I came across bright shining lies every day.

My original plan after the navy was to go to law school. But I was then twenty-seven years old, and I thought, "Oh God, I'll be thirty before I do anything." I had college classmates who had gone to law school and were clerking at the Supreme Court; people I knew were doing all kinds of interesting things, and I thought, "Thirty is too late." At that time, thirty was thought to be a real demarcation line.

It dawned on me that journalism might be a good profession. It appealed to a curiosity and obsession about finding the truth that had been building up in me over the years.

I lived in Washington, about six blocks from the offices of the *Washington Post*. With the fearlessness and naiveté of youth, I walked into the newsroom, found Harry Rosenfeld, the metropolitan editor, and said, "I think I'd like to take a crack at journalism." My experience was pretty thin: I'd worked at the Yale Banner, which put out the yearbooks and other college publications. But the president of the *Post* at the time, Paul Ignatius, had been secretary of the navy and, because of my service, he recommended that I be given a shot. So they gave me a two-week tryout.

I wrote a dozen stories, none of which were published and none of which were much good. Rosenfeld finally told me, "You know, you don't know how to do this." And I said, "I agree, but thanks for the chance because I realize that this is what I really want to do." So he helped me get a job at the *Montgomery County Sentinel*, a weekly paper in Montgomery County, Maryland, just north of Washington.

I worked at the *Sentinel* for a year and loved it. I wrote a number of stories that were picked up by the *Washington Post*, one making the front page of the *Post* and one making the front page of the *New York Times*. A couple of *Post* reporters who covered Montgomery County told Rosenfeld that I was scooping them and that he ought to hire me, which he did, in September 1971. I joined the *Post* on the same day that future Watergate figures Howard Hunt and Gordon Liddy got on a flight from Washington to Los Angeles to break into the office of antiwar activist Daniel Ellsberg's psychiatrist. Of course, I didn't know it at the time, but it's one of those ironies of convergence.

My first assignment at the *Post* was the night police beat, and I loved it. Then, nine months later, on June 17, 1972, the burglary at the Democratic National Committee headquarters at the Watergate apartment complex took place. It was a beautiful Saturday and a lot of the veteran reporters didn't want to come in to cover what initially looked like a petty crime. The city editor called me, and I, of course, went right in. Carl Bernstein also leapt at the assignment. We had no more than a passing acquaintance at the time and were quite distrustful of each other.

The Nixon administration, of course, immediately denied any involvement in what they labeled a third-rate crime. I applied my skeptical mindset to their denials. My and Carl's work on the story, one piece of the puzzle, one article at a time—with the full-throttle support of the *Post*'s executive editor, Ben Bradlee, and its owner, Katherine Graham—culminated in Nixon resigning the presidency on August 9, 1974.

A determination to tell the truth has driven me since those days. No one, certainly not me, gets it right all the time. But we get misinformation from leaders and our government continuously, and I think journalists have a responsibility to correct it.

my mother's family ever attended college, they were adventurous, resourceful, and entrepreneurial people.

My father grew up in one of the poorest mining towns in West Virginia. His large family lived in a two-room house; babies arrived, relatives came to live for extended periods, and there was rarely enough to eat. When my grandfather abandoned his wife and kids, my grandmother, unable to care for all her children, was forced to send some of them away. As a result, my father spent part of his childhood in an orphanage. The family struggled to survive, keep food on the table, and a fire in the stove.

In retrospect, the closest I ever came to thinking about my future was dreaming of becoming a professional baseball player. I used to listen to the New York Yankees games on a staticky transistor radio in my bedroom in Virginia. Mickey Mantle was my hero. Even as I was projecting myself onto those distant diamonds, I knew my dreams were unrealistic.

As it turned out, athletics played a pivotal role in my life, even if not in the way I'd fantasized.

My brother and I attended Washington-Lee High School in Arlington, Virginia. I loved sports, and by my senior year, I'd become good friends with the football coach and athletic director, a charismatic man named John C. Youngblood. Hundreds of students looked up to him; he became my role model. I began to think I could become an athletic director like him, maybe even at the college level. For fifteen years after high school, I stuck to a game plan: I majored in physical education in college and graduated to become a teacher and head football coach at the junior high I'd attended as a teenager. A few years later, I got a master's degree and at an early age became assistant athletic director at George Washington University.

After five years at GW, the athletic director announced his retirement, and I was assured of taking his place. Then Harry Rhoads sent that fateful article from *Fortune* magazine suggesting we start a lecture agency.

When we received our friend's half-serious note attached to that magazine article, Paula took it seriously. I thought she had to be joking and dismissed the whole idea. I was on the path I'd been following since high school, and it was paying off. I was following the plans I'd laid out with John years earlier.

Paula pressed me on it. She'd seen ways in which I was frustrated by being unable to institute ideas I had for the university's athletic department. In education, even college athletics, committees run most everything, and committees tend to be political and a lot more talk than action. I knew she was right, but I'd learned to live with it.

And then she reminded me of something that had happened years earlier. As a graduate student, I'd worked as assistant director of a local community swimming pool. It was a good job, and the summer income was important to pay for graduate school. About once a week, usually a Friday or Saturday, we would keep the staff after closing and have a few beers. It wasn't exactly allowed, but the director of the pool, who I had known since I was twelve, saw it as a morale booster and looked the other way. One night we decided to invite more friends than usual. About an hour into the party, a member of the board who lived nearby noticed the overhead pool lights and called the pool director. When he arrived, he closed down the party. I was fired the next day.

Although I routinely dismissed the incident and had, over the years, my share of laughs about it, Paula understood I was troubled by it. She knew I'd never really be happy unless my success or failure was in my own hands. "You will never be truly happy or confident in your future, if you can't make your own decisions and control your own destiny," she told me.

As it turned out, Paula was doing more than offering me career advice; she was articulating the very philosophy that would define our greatest success—the very essence of entrepreneurial spirit.

It was Paula's vision that had helped me see John Youngblood's true gift. It wasn't that he'd given me a blueprint; he'd inspired me to believe in myself. When I was able to do that, I was able to see my life with unlimited possibilities, where preposterous ideas can be dreams come true.

I owe a lot to John Youngblood—he was that defining teacher we all hope for in life. But I owe the most to Paula. Paula saw a life for me that I would have never imagined for myself. Her insight, vision, and persistence singlehandedly changed my life at just the perfect time, opening up a brand new world for me. Without Paula, the Washington Speakers Bureau would have never existed and this book would have never been written and all these stories might never have been told.

Recognizing the transformational moments in your life is a powerful experience. I can attest to that.

ABOUT THE AUTHOR

Bernie Swain is co-founder and Chairman of Washington Speakers Bureau.

Swain grew up in Arlington, VA. His high school athletic director inspired him to pursue a career in college athletics; he earned his undergraduate and master's degrees from George Washington University, where he met his wife, Paula.

Swain subsequently joined the University's athletic department, and he and Paula started a family.

Swain spent the next five years preparing to take over the job of Athletic Director. But just as his boss was ready to retire and promote him, Swain abruptly quit to join Paula and friend Harry Rhoads to start a lecture agency—without experience, without a plan, and without a single client.

What happened next is a classic American success story.

The three co-founders started Washington Speakers Bureau from a small supply closet belonging to Chuck Hagel, who would later become Secretary of Defense. One rocky year later, just as their savings was running out, Swain secured their first speaker and hastily sealed the deal with a handshake. This gesture became WSB's defining moment: The trio recruited more speakers. Word spread that a new lecture agency was in town—and was growing fast on the strength of its handshake. Indeed, eight short years later, their roster of speakers had far exceeded the industry leader's. WSB was now established as the top lecture agency in the world.

WSB's growth and reputation has continued to expand. Over the last thirty-five years, the agency has represented three US Presidents, four prime ministers of Great Britain, countless American and world leaders, business and economic visionaries, journalists, authors, and sports legends.

Today, Swain remains Chairman of Washington Speakers Bureau. He and Paula have been married forty-two years; they have three children, Tim, Michael, and Kelley.

For more, visit BernieSwain.com.